Praise for A M
from Tragedy to Triumph

"Again, this is not just a story. Come along and see an actual glimpse of the glory of God. Salvation is the gift of the beginning...but there is more. God is great, faithful, and good. Come along and be taken into his gift of love."

Susanna DeLosSantos

"Many readers will relate to the struggles that Rita Hinton so candidly shares in this work. Having endured a similar experience with our daughter at the age of nine, reading Rita's words was a familiar yet indescribable journey. This precious book is filled with vivid images, beautiful phrasing, and honest emotion.

As I read this book and revisited my own desperate experience with our seriously ill child, I was able to rejoice with the Hinton family as they found victory through this tremendous ordeal. We too have experienced this blessed victory as our daughter turned thirteen this month! Praise God for his miraculous healing power!"

Kim Cullen

"The book is wonderful. A true miracle has

taken place. This is the testimony of a mother's unshakable faith in her Lord and Savior and of a loving supportive husband, a true man of God, who also has such a faith…in his wife as well. I know you will love their story."

Hedy Diossy
Author of *A Promise*

"Come along and experience a story of faith and obedience. As I read the book I was captivated and felt that I was on the scene when the miracle was taking place. This first-hand experience told wonderfully by Rita Hinton is an encouragement to those who are looking for God in the midst of despair."

Dr. Larry M. Baucom
Pastor, Sarasota Suncoast Community Church

a MIRACLE *of* LOVE

a MIRACLE *of* LOVE

TURNING FROM
TRAGEDY TO TRIUMPH

by Rita Hinton

Tate Publishing & Enterprises

A Miracle of Love: Turning from Tragedy to Triumph

This title is also available as a Tate Out Loud product. Visit www.tatepublishing.com for more information.

The opinions expressed by the author are not necessarily those of Tate Publishing, LLC.

This book contains descriptions of situations and events that are recounted as accurately as possible from the author's memory. The names of those involved may have been changed in order to protect their privacy.

Published by Tate Publishing & Enterprises, LLC
127 E. Trade Center Terrace | Mustang, Oklahoma 73064 USA
1.888.361.9473 | www.tatepublishing.com

Tate Publishing is committed to excellence in the publishing industry. The company reflects the philosophy established by the founders, based on Psalm 68:11,
"The Lord gave the word and great was the company of those who published it."

Cover design by Jonathan Lindsey
Interior design by Kandi Evans

Published in the United States of America

ISBN: 978-1-60604-858-0
1. Inspiriational Christian Living, Memoir
2. Miracles, Legalism, Freedom
08.01.08

TO MY BELOVED CHILDREN,
ROBERT, RHIANNA, RICHIE, RITA,
RONEL, AND RONNY.

Table of Contents

Foreword

To a man, the title *A Miracle of Love* may not sound masculine or tough-guyish enough.

Do not be fooled! This little book will take you through the "valley of the shadow of death" to the glorious mountaintop of God's power. I have experienced this story first hand, being the husband of the author and the father of our Richie boy.

I am writing this foreword years later, with the wisdom of hindsight. The rewards that our changed lives produced began back then. We have progressed steadily from glory to glory, from strength to strength ever since.

My guess is that a woman will "get" this message intuitively, as did the many who read the first edition. But this foreword is written with you in mind, sir, who probably received this book from your wife or female friend. It's okay. Read it and get the benefits this book offers, as you look at the turning point in the life of a fellow man, who did not think there was any need for such a turning.

I used to sit in church week after week, thinking that I was doing my duty, taking care of the family. I considered myself a good dad and a faithful husband and even enjoyed my role, most of the time. Then one day, the little faith I had was called on, and the man inside was shaken to the core. The drama was gut wrenching. Even to this day, the memory is hard to relive. However, to come out on the other side of the valley—revived in my relationship with God and with my wife, which is getting better every day—made the short time of absolute darkness valuable, when considering the big picture.

My hope for you, friend, is that you read this story as if this was an invitation to you to grow your faith or as if this was a potential turning point for you also. Find the living God, and if you already have a relationship with God, discover more of the Eternal One, who is the conqueror of death and the giver and restorer of life; the One who revives true love in the soul of man. May your heart be richly blessed and refreshed.

Rich Hinton
Former Major League baseball player
President R.M. Hinton Construction Inc.
Co-founder of First Love Revival Ministries

Introduction to Our Sacred Story

What does it take to turn from tragedy to triumph? What does it take to turn from hopelessness to sure hope? How does one turn from a desperate state of lacking, to the overflow of true love? Can make-believe religion be transformed into a genuine relationship with the living God?

This true story was written with the intent to offer you an opportunity to come up with your answers to the above questions. While contemplating the authentic account of our miracle, some readers could find the notions offered here astonishing.

When I say "this was not luck!" be assured, the author is not trying to solicit agreement with her conclusions. This is not a crusade to win anybody over to believe in miracles. Nevertheless, I do hope to offer enrichment of faith to each of you with this writing. The potential benefits are very real when hearing, or as it is in this case reading, about our experience is enough to affect a life-change.

Over the years, we have received plenteous feedback, attesting to the valuable insights that this story offers to those looking for answers in perplexing situations.

By now we are sure that not everybody has to go through something like we did to awaken from the comatose state of "going through the motions" that characterize our human existence at times. This kind of shaking is not necessary for all; however, all of us are called at one time or another, to wake up and start walking toward a life truly worth living.

Maybe you are ready to get up and move forward on your journey. Maybe somebody gave you this book, hoping to encourage you to have faith for the "impossible" in the midst of a challenging situation. Whatever your "impossible-s" are, take this opportunity to get a fresh vision of what Christ meant, when he said, "With men this is impossible, but *with God all things are possible*" (Matthew 19:26, NKJV, emphasis added).

With utmost goodwill, you are invited to read and to hear the message of divine revelation…for you too. That is how it starts; with an attentive ear and a willing heart we perceive the eternal call to the personal encounter that only God can orchestrate. It is my privilege to satisfy the requests to write about our experience and to accommodate those who wanted to make our story available to a larger readership.

Not that I have nothing else to do; there is still plenty on my plate being a mother of six. The children are not grown and not gone from the nest. The house is still full of their wonderful presence. How do I find time to write? I do not find it—I take it!

I could be sleeping now; it is way too early to be up…but the "urge is upon me," without which I would not even try to do anything of this sort. Being bilingual, sometimes it is a challenge for me to express what I am thinking about in another tongue (which provides my teenagers with a lot of fuel for laughter and teasing). They delight in reminding me that I am not supposed to be an author, and I do not argue with them. Actually I was the one who proclaimed with utmost certainty that I could never be a writer of books, or be a speaker, because of my stubborn accent, (that my children lovingly refer to as "a speech impediment").

Yet here we are, years later; I am doing the

impossible-s with supreme enjoyment, well aware that anything I say or write has value only because of God, who set out to prove his power in my weaknesses. Therefore, I am confident that if what I am sensing is God's prompting, then I will have no struggles writing this book. My fingers will fly over the keys, and this will be a most exciting and worthwhile investment of my time. I know because it happened before. God and I have written "together" in the past. On such occasions, my uncertainty is swept away and I know I can do it, even in the face of opposition.

I remember before I started my first book, a short allegory with the long title, *Your Invitation to Timeless Joy—RSVP,* God taught me an important principle about overcoming opposition. My daring mission to author a book was nearly abandoned because of an incredulous "expert's" reaction to my secret project. After I let her in on what I thought was God's prompting, she actually asked me: "Who do you think you are?" Now I don't know about you, but in my world, a question like that can give one a big bouquet of mixed emotions.

Yeah, who did I think I was? I wondered silently studying the expert's countenance. A part of me was about to agree with her, so I had to make a quick decision whether I should join her sentiment or crack up laughing. For a moment it seemed so logical to give up the "silly idea" of being inspired by God. I nearly misunderstood too and was about to scoff at my ability to write for the benefit of others because a part of me took the dissuasion seriously...but not for long. After we shared a good-natured snicker, I had an encouraging insight.

You see, "Who do I think I am?" is really not the deciding factor. It can be a hindrance to dwell on such thoughts if we have habitually limited ourselves based on what others say. The determining question is: "Who do I think my God is?" That is what matters most when it comes to doing things against all odds or contrary to the permission of the experts.

The only ingredient I needed to start writing was willingness to believe that God would actually be so wonderful to not only inspire, but also enable me to produce a book that is proving to be a "life-changer" to more and more readers.

May I encourage you to apply this principle also before reading this account? Maybe you are questioning yourself about what you can or cannot do. Allow this story to serve you by facilitating an inquiry into your desires and possibilities. Who knows, you might get a glimpse of the big picture of your abilities and also get the needed assistance from a source that you have not yet tapped into.

"Your books are working miracles!" is a reoccurring comment from readers, indicating that the content of our books can hit home in a personal way. Whether you "get it" or not is up to you. I have attempted to follow the true Author's instructions, and the rest is between you and God.

Producing this book was a very unique experience. This is not an allegory...there is no fiction here. Even though it was a tremendously challenging project, it proved to be a very worthwhile investment of my time and emotion. Because this was a co-creative process, there is a lot more to this work than sharing our memories. There was a lot of reliving, healing, and "soaring in joy" while creating this book. May it be so for you too as you read on.

My hope is that you will partake of this story in God's perfect timing to lift your heart and soul to new realms of faith and trust. Our testimony is a living proof that can serve as an example of how anybody can turn from tragedy to triumph in the love of God.

May our sacred story benefit you greatly! May it be an encouragement amidst the impossible moments and circumstances of your life. Remember, what God does for one, God can and will do for others...for you too!

And if, after finishing this story, you still have some questions about how to enter into an authentic relationship with the Almighty, there is a bonus section in the back that will spell it out for you step by step. In the meantime be blessed by the atmosphere of perfect love surrounding you as you read.

Rita Hinton
First Love Revival Ministries

Sometimes God . . .

It was Christmas season; once again the children were practicing for the play. Organized by age and height, the little clumps of lively boys and girls seemed to fill the sanctuary. A huge, dark-blue piece of paper was put up between the choir loft and the baptistery to cover the back of the platform, giving the illusion of great distance. It was quite clever: the blinking lights punched through the paper gave the appearance of a night sky with sparkling stars, creating an atmosphere of mystery and wonder. Palm trees and paper camels added to the delight of the little ones who beheld such an amazing sight for the first time.

The moms were sitting in the pews trying to keep up with conversations while coaching their darlings in the limelight.

As I looked around in the dimly lit sanctuary,

greeting the other mothers sitting spread out in the room, my eyes rested on the row I sat in the Sunday before.

Something was triggered in my memory. I remembered the sermon vaguely; it was good, challenging, but what was it about?

"Sometimes God..." What was it? I searched in my mind. I remembered praying about something in a kind of fervency, but what was it that touched me so to pray with such fervency? How could I forget?

Oh well, that's just how it is these days...probably the pregnancy...after all, I am in my eighth month with my fourth child, and it is difficult to try to be super mom. If these people knew what I go through every day just to get out of bed, they would feel so sorry for me; but I could not let that happen.

People feeling sorry for me—that was one thing I could not stand. It did not fit with the way I wanted to be seen by my peers.

I shifted my eyes away from that spot and glanced around to see where my little ones were. So prim and proper, dressed color-coded from head to toe, hair in perfect order, immovably gelled into place. Even the eighteen-month-old looked like one of those model babies from a magazine. How adorable he looked with his little suspenders as he tried to mingle with the "big boys" on the stairs of the stage.

His older brother, my first born, and his older sister attempted to chase him off, but he would stand his ground and pretend to be one of them in the play.

The teacher did not mind his presence, and I was more than willing to let him have his fun with the others instead of forcing him to sit with me and watch. He was so full of life and so hungry to experience everything that the moment offered. A most delightful child, he was so lovable with his shy smile and sparkling blue eyes. We called him King Richard, the explorer, for obvious reasons to all of us who knew him. He was into everything…fearlessly exploring every nook and corner of his expanding world, which put a lot of miles on my feet as I was constantly trying to catch up with him.

Feeling exhausted already, I tried to put my swollen feet up as often as possible, to obey the doctor's orders. But what can one do in a pew? Changing positions did not give me the much-wanted relief. Nothing really helped these days. Comfort escaped me with every desperate attempt to forget my bulging belly. Finally, I settled down closer to the stage so I could keep an eye on all the children practicing their entry into the first scene.

My thoughts ran in a circular pattern about the days ahead of me. *How am I going to handle all this?* I would agonize in the secret place of my tormented mind. I could not imagine one more thing added to my already full plate. The baby would soon be born. My time of confinement loomed on the horizon once again with sleepless nights and the intensity of caring for another addition to our family.

Don't get me wrong—I loved my babies, and I was very thankful for them. But at the same time, each new life brought a tremendous challenge to live beyond the edge of what I ever thought possible.

There were moments when I just wanted to run. Not from my family, but from the overwhelming multitasking lifestyle that I found myself in that was increasing in intensity with each child with no relief in sight for many years to come. Can anyone relate?

There was nowhere to run, and I had a reputation—a hard-earned name among my peers—to maintain. It was good to be thought of as "such a good mother, so patient, so gentle, and so courageous to have all these children." And, of course, all this was credited to the great faith and strong loyalty to God that I appeared to have.

Not that I tried to deceive anybody, but I did

not know any better than to pretend to live a life that, at least on the surface, seemed right. I did not know about the life of a completely different nature and purpose...not yet!

I thought I was doing my best under the circumstances. Trying to maintain the picture of our family functioning well seemed my Christian duty. It was all about keeping up a front, never admitting being overwhelmed, because, after all, we were supposed to be "trusting in the Lord." Forcing my family into the mold that I perceived as the expectation of the church was my most disappointing and exhausting task. Nobody knew about the civil war that was going on in my soul.

The battles between fear, trust, pride, and love were raging continually, not only in my soul, but in my closest relationships as well. Mistakenly, I thought this is what fighting the "good fight" meant. I was out to change my husband and children into "happy Christians," even if it killed them!

Based on my observations of other "happy Christians," I made a faulty conclusion that to fake it is acceptable as long as we try really hard to get to the reality of that much desired "life in Christ" one day. Because of not understanding what it took to get there, we were in constant struggles, exerting vain efforts to measure up to the ever-changing standards of well-meaning counselors.

If you have heard me speak at an event recently, you may be asking, "But I thought you were wonderfully changed when you met Christ...what happened? When did that wonder and awe cease to burn in your heart? How did that first love, that joyful sense of newness slip away?" Let me explain in a few short sentences.

Most of the time my speeches are timed and, to do justice to this episode of my life, I usually don't go into this experience unless I am granted more time to clarify how this could happen to someone so drastically "saved."

Coming to Christ was the very best step I have ever taken. Forgiveness, cleansing, restoration, and love were granted from God, and I have thankfully embraced the message of salvation in Jesus Christ. This really transformed my outlook, and it was clear that my life was working out for the best. There was such excitement and joy in those early years.

At first, I wanted everyone to have this newfound life. My loved ones were on the "hit list," and to "get them saved" became the purpose of my every waking moment. Then something went wrong...but what?

I tried to do everything right. We joined a church and I followed all the rules that the leaders and counselors pointed out. I read my Bible daily, even if I was too tired to concentrate. I did this to ensure that I stayed in good standing with God. And, "for their own good," I demanded that my children and husband did the same. He was supposed to be the spiritual leader, it was his duty—so I heard—to live up to these simple rules. And my "duty" was to help him do what he did not feel like doing.

We argued about his neglected "call" constantly. But in public he played his part as I played mine, pretending to be his "helpmate," whatever that was supposed to mean.

Our children memorized, recited, and behaved. My heart ached under this entire facade. The longing after true happiness was to be suppressed in order to achieve the "holiness that was much more important to God than our happiness"—so we heard. Deep down, all I wanted was just to love my family like I used to—before these doctrines were laid on us—with the kind of love that was now labeled the "spoiling kind of human love." Then why didn't I just reject those hindering dogmas?

The problem was that these doctrines worked...no question about it.

We were stopped at restaurants as we walked by admiring patrons, telling us what a wonderful sight our family was to behold. "Such obedient children!" They would comment on our appearance, and we would be pleased. But when I looked into my children's eyes, I could see exasperation and suppression. They had to behave or else. "For their own good" they were drilled and trained to have acceptable behavior until there was not a second left in their waking moments just to be children.

Did love drive me into this kind of parenting? Hardly. The warmth of human, instinctive love was covered over with the cold tablets of man-made tenets that served as the prescriptions of successful parenting.

Was this kind of Christianity God's will? Not at all! But we did not know any better. The simple desire to be good turned into a dread of falling short of God's expectations. This fear motivated me to strive hard for a life that was dictated by the rules and traditions of man instead of God. Strict adherence to the endless laws and regulations seemed the only security for me and my family. The more like a controlling monster I felt, the more confused I became with God. What kind of God did I believe in anyway? I started to wonder if I really wanted to please him that much anymore.

What happened to that wonderful Savior who died to eradicate my wrongdoings and to transform me into that new person who would love like

He did? Was this all there was to the "abundant life" that we were supposed to have in Christ?

That sermon on Sunday addressed this concern of mine, and it perked me up for a moment. A statement stirred me deeply. In a scary but very urgent way, the message was calling me to climb out of the ditch into which I had fallen.

What ditch? The ditch of man-made religiosity, a place of deadly inertia, a place of false security where good works earned the favor with God.

How did I get there? Quite gradually, little by little...here a little, there a little, allowing others to tell me about God rather than finding out myself what I needed to know to have the good life in Christ.

So here I was, in the dimly lit sanctuary, searching in my memory, trying to bring back the content of that stirring message that seemed to echo in my heart with an insistent cry for freedom.

My mind was distracted by the activities around me, but I kept searching in my purse for the sermon outline that I remembered taking notes on during the Sunday service.

I remembered scribbling on a yellow slip of paper while I was listening to the preacher. "Sometimes God...allows..." I mused but could not recall what the rest of that statement was.

I looked around in my bag; my Bible was among

the diapers, bottles, and toys I dragged along with me everywhere we went. *Surely that outline is still in there,* I thought as I rummaged around quite unaware of the children walking by me on their way to the platform.

"Hi, Mommy!" I heard my big boy whisper.

"Hi, Mommy!" My daughter's sweet voice caught my attention.

I looked up, watching them march around the corner of my pew; I wondered where the littlest one was in the lineup. He must be there somewhere. He was much shorter than the rest of the troops. Maybe he has hid behind the benches, I figured. Just to make sure, I stood up laboriously to check among the children's heads bobbing up and down in the aisle. No, he was not with them. He was probably on one of his explorations. I thought I had better go and get him before he pulled down some of the decorations.

I waddled slowly off, calling his name softly to not interfere with the rehearsal in progress.

Where could he be? I wondered as my eyes searched the whole sanctuary systematically. He could not be hiding under the benches. Did he fall asleep in a corner? No, there is no way. His love for people and the fun they were having would not let him stay away from the real action with the others. But where is he? I exchanged a knowing smile with the other mothers as they saw me looking for my little adventurer.

Behind the stage were the choir loft and the baptistery with the dressing rooms. There were two sets of stairways leading up to the baptismal pool, one side for the ladies and the other for the men. Because of the play, all the choir chairs were stacked up in the back of the stage, practically blockading the entire area that was illuminated with nothing but one fire-exit light above the back door.

A thought occurred as I walked past the big paper wall: *"Don't go there! That is the wrong way! It is way too dark back there. No baby would dare to go there."*

I looked up into the stairway leading up to the baptism pool. It was pitch dark, but I called his name anyway and took a few steps behind the scene.

"You have no business being here!" This was a rather menacing notion in my mind. *"Get out! Someone will think you are snooping around!"*

These were suggestions that pushed every button in my nature to retreat, but for some unexplainable reason I kept walking into the dark. After going around full circle behind the choir loft among the stacked up chairs, I came to the other side of the baptistery stairs. Again I looked up and assured myself that he could not possibly be up there, so I was about to turn around when instead I stepped upward into the thick darkness.

There was an ominous stillness.

"What am I doing? What will they think if somebody finds me here, in the dark, on the men's side of the dressing rooms?"

In spite of all these bombarding thoughts, I kept walking upward to the top of the stairs.

"Get off! Get out of here!" What on earth was happening in my head?

Never before have I experienced such outright, vicious thoughts whirling in my mind.

Sometimes God... Allows...

My eyes were getting used to the darkness now. The silence was deafening. To this day it is hard to put all of this together to make sense in my mind. Just a few feet from where I was standing on the other side of the paper wall, the rehearsal was in full swing with music and singing. But I remember this moment as total screaming silence. I peeked toward the baptism tub. As I strained my eyes, the picture of the Jordan River painted on the backdrop became dimly visible. The water was perfectly still and black in the shadows.

But what was that? A robe or towel or something was left in there, floating on the surface in the center of the pool.

Well, it was none of my business. I was about to turn around when I took another look.

As if a lightning-bolt struck me from the top

of my head down to my toes, an almost unbearable pain hit me in every part of my being.

What followed was a series of movements that were beyond my abilities and strength. I threw myself into the water, grabbed my precious son's body with one hand, and leaped upward with one continuous motion. I do not remember how I came down those stairs with my drenched clothes or how I passed through those chairs piled up in the dark. His limp body was hanging head down, dangling from side to side with every stride.

A young man was close to the door and jumped back in terror as he realized what he saw.

"Help!" I pleaded, but he froze with eyes as round as saucers.

I ran past him through the double doors leading out of the sanctuary, not to interfere with the rehearsal. (Yes, not wanting to cause the agenda of the day to be interrupted, I took our disaster outside.)

Once in the foyer, I laid my baby on the floor and pleaded with the shocked onlookers.

"Help! Get Help!" But nobody moved.

"Lord!" I called out in desperation. Finally, a woman from the sound room ran to the phone.

"Lord!" I kept calling from then on. Somehow nothing else came to my lips. "Lord!" I called upward like never before. "Lord!" I needed to be heard. "Lord!" Surrounded by more and more people, I realized that there was no hope but in God. I understood that unless God steps in, there was no help in that lonely place. As I kept calling out to God, each time I pushed on my baby's body.

"Breathe!" I heard my voice pleading before turning to God again.

One of the young mothers who was a nurse came out of the sanctuary, threw herself at our side, and began CPR.

I looked up. There was a woman in front of me with her eyes closed. She was praying, completely absorbed. She wasn't watching; she was praying! What comfort that sight gave me. I felt a surge of hope as I looked at her.

Another woman knelt beside me and whispered: "Come, you must rest. Don't watch this! Come, let go of him now; it is cold here." Without words my body spoke to her: "No…no…I can't do that!" Doesn't she know? I can't let go. I must hold on to him.

The nurse was working diligently, giving gentle little puffs when we heard a gurgling exhalation. We were energized with indescribable joy and kept at it until we heard the ambulance arrive.

The EMT ran in and started to cut his clothes off him. Quickly, I took off his suspenders before the scissors got there. These were the one with the race cars—his favorite ones. He would enjoy them again, I felt assured, as soon as he will recover from all this. Very soon this nightmare will be over and everything will be as it used to be. I heard him exhale—he was not dead! He was in the hands of the professionals. They will just bring him back, and we will forget that this ever happened.

Little did I know what was ahead, and I had no clue of the greater plan that was about to unfold and change us forever.

My baby was breathing through a tube, placed on a stretcher, and whisked away to be stabilized for transport. I stood by the ambulance with his cut up clothes, trying to get a glimpse through the window. I refused to go home to change clothes. It was bitter cold, but I could not care.

The pastor joined us outside, and he seemed to read my tormented mind. He said, "Now, don't start blaming yourself! You didn't do this to him! God is in control here, and he will work it all out. You will see!"

My dear friend, the nurse who breathed those promising puffs of life into my boy's body, offered to drive me to the hospital where the ambulance was headed. We followed the vehicle speeding through the traffic with sirens blaring. She was courageously weaving through the traffic and talking the whole time, even though I never gave her an answer. Something was shut off in me. I had no idea what she was saying. I could not register or respond to her words.

I became aware of an eye in my being—an eye that was looking upward even when faced with people and in spite of the rapid changes in my surroundings. Maybe this is normal for others, but I did not know before this experience that I could keep such a focus toward another realm—the realm of faith. I realized that I had to keep this focus so as to not fall into despair. At my right side there was a huge black hole, like a gaping mouth waiting for me to look down into it. But this eye that was looking upward kept me away from it. Somehow this eye was committed to keep looking up, and that is the only thing that mattered right now.

"Just don't look away into the darkness" was the fervent encouragement of this eye. I could not talk or listen to others. I had to keep that upward look.

My driver was gracious. She understood my silence and kept talking anyway. My wet clothes were soaking her car seat, but she did not care. Such a wonderful friend! How I love her to this day. How beautiful she is to me. A faithful friend she is, sent by God to be there in such a selfless way.

How could this happen? What have I done to deserve this? Why is God punishing me in such a horrible way? These questions were crowding at the gate of my mind, but I would not let them in. None of it!

I kept recalling my pastor's words. "You did not do this! God is in control!"

Good words! Practical words…useful words…helpful words! Did I believe them? No, but I had no other alternative than to hope that they were true. They strengthened my resolve to keep looking upward from where my help was to come.

Something started to stir in the depth of my soul.

The emergency room was filled with doctors, nurses, and sympathetic patients who forgot their plight for a moment as they watched our drama. I was allowed to be near my son, trying to warm his ice-cold feet. I remember the somber faces, shaking heads, a nurse with a golden cross on her neck with her tears running down her face…my lonely voice calling on the Lord for every breath for my baby. Our pediatrician arrived, and the doctors exchanged glances. I was tempted to turn toward that blackness at that moment. The physician shone a light into my little one's eyes. It was a strange sight. What happened to his blue eyes? Where was the blue? It was all black. What happened?

"Lord!" I called and looked upward again.

The doctor's shaking hands could not find a vein. In frustration, he gave up.

"Are they ready?" he yelled. "We have to lift him to All Children's..."

Okay, I thought, I'll go with him on the helicopter, but they said no.

By now my husband arrived. He was miraculously found by one of the moms from church who had tried to find him in a neighborhood where she thought he was working. She prayed to be led to the construction site where he was building a house, and she found him right away.

He was pale and desperate when he arrived at the emergency room. And he was just in time to peel me off our boy so they could take him to the helicopter launching pad on the top of the hospital roof.

Trembling, he leaned over and prayed into our placid baby's ear, as he lay there all bundled up and ready to go.

He prayed into my ear, too. He assured me that we would go as fast as possible and see him soon. He assured me that God was watching over our baby while we were apart for that short time. It was about a forty-five minute drive to get to the Children's Hospital.

My husband also insisted that we go home so I

could change. My knit outfit was holding the water well, and I was shivering uncontrollably by now. He gently but firmly led, and I submitted without a stir of self-will left in me.

As we drove home in complete silence, an interesting change took place in my thoughts. A well-known verse from the Bible entered into my mind and took over: *"All things work together for good..."*

What was the rest of it? There was more to this verse...something else...a condition...I remembered a stern teaching on that. What was the condition to have things work out for good? I searched in my memory bank, but all I could remember was how disappointed I had been listening to a lady lecturing on this subject and how very disqualified I felt after she was finished expounding on our utter lack to deserve any favors from God. I remembered nodding in agreement then. However, now it was of utmost importance to find some real answers.

If there was any way in which I could affect this to work out for good, I needed to know. No more hearsay! I needed to find out what God said, not the interpretation. Where was my Bible?

At home we changed quickly and quietly, packed a few things, and were ready to go when I noticed my bag with my Bible that someone from church dropped off at our house. Just before we left for the hospital a phone call assured us that our older children were with a precious woman and her family—the very best choice under the circumstances. As I walked past the children's room, Winnie the Pooh "looked" at me, wanting to go, too. I grabbed the favorite stuffed friend of our little one and off we sped into the unknown.

. . . *A Hopeless Situation* . . .

Neither one of us could talk as we drove to the hospital. The inward battle raged on for my attention, but it was very distinctly only on the periphery of my mind. Somehow a peace settled over me, and no thought could disturb the core of my being. A cocoon of peace…that is what it felt like…quite strange yet so welcome.

There was no need to ask questions or to clarify how it happened. I remember being very thankful for that. My husband did not need me to tell him anything.

Then I realized that neither of us shed a tear. How strange…how utterly strange everything seemed. The world was still going on. People laughed, worked, ate, and played as we rushed by them, in our car, on our way to be with our little one. It did not make sense.

The world did not turn for me anymore. It came to a dead stop, and everything that made life wonderful did not fit anymore.

Not that I was upset at people. I just could not understand how they could go on. I remember looking at a passenger in another car as we sped past his vehicle on the highway. His smile froze as he glanced at me, and he turned his head away quickly. What did he see? I did not know, but after similar encounters with other faces, I resolved not to meet another eye with mine. What contorted my face into such a shocking sight was my private experience. What is the point invading another life—for whom the world was still turning—with my doldrums and the slow motion of every thought? Emotionally we were kept in a strange peace that we needed more than we understood at the time.

Everything seemed too fast on the outside. It hurt to have to think fast. We needed comfort and for now we have found it in stillness.

At the hospital we were told that we needed to meet with a counselor of some sort before we could see our son. We were ushered into a plush, cozy room with dim lights and a sense of isolation from the noisy world of the busy hospital corridor.

The counselor talked very softly and slowly. He must have known that we were in that "slow, quiet place" for now and that rushing words could not have gotten through to our minds. He spoke about tragedies and coping and decision-making. I heard the words, but they did not connect at all. Every word was by itself, separated from the next. I had never known of such a state of mind, so I sat there amazed at what was happening. He asked a question, but neither of us could answer.

Did he ask my name? Bewildered, my husband and I looked at each other then back at him. We were at a loss. What amazed me was that he seemed to understand. He waited.

Finally, something connected together in my mind, so almost excited I blurted it out: "Everything is going to work out for good! God will work it all out!" I heard my voice and felt as if the wall spoke the words.

The counselor's mouth moved again. As much as I tried to concentrate on what he said, I could not hear it as a sentence. So I responded with the same statement back to him. There was nothing else I could put together. He looked at me, then at my husband, folded his clipboard as if he had nothing else to say, and left the room.

Did he give up on trying to comfort us? Why did he leave so quickly? Were we a hopeless case? Did we offend him?

We just sat there in the plush silence for a while but nothing happened.

"Let's go," my husband said slowly. "We will see him now."

We searched for the place but could not find our baby. Finally, my husband grabbed a phone on the wall and kept pushing the buttons until we got directions to the intensive care unit. A doctor and nurse met us and explained to us that they had "good news" and not-so-good news.

The good news was that during the transport on the helicopter our son started to cry and breathe on his own. The other part of the information we needed to know was that he would have a long recovery. He was in bad shape; therefore, we would have to move into the Ronald McDonald House for an extended time before we could take him home. But we should be happy! He had been near death, but he was not dead. So now we should start making arrangements for the coming months ahead. That is why the counselor was sent to help us rearrange our lives and work out the details.

There was more good news. We could stay at the Ronald McDonald House for free. These words were like giant drops exploding on my mind. I could handle those about him crying and breathing on his own, but the rest were too much.

I was gasping for air; my chest was so tight I could hardly breathe.

No! I don't want that! No! Don't say that. No, I cannot stay here. I cannot leave my other children at home and I cannot leave my little one here. No! I cannot accept this! I groaned inwardly. As if kicking desperately to keep afloat above these words and the pictures they were creating in my imagination, my attention was slipping toward that dark hole that I had refused to look into so far.

"I can't handle this," I heard myself repeating. I felt so forlorn again.

A phone call interrupted this slippery moment. Our pastor called to find out what was going on. I told him what we were just informed about. He could hear where I was heading emotionally, and he—of all things—rebuked me!

Yes, it was a kind of slap in the face to prevent one from passing out. In his firm and fatherly voice he said, "Now listen to me…you stop that! You believe God is in control of this, right? Then, don't make an impression on those who are watching you like you don't trust him. Think of your testimony!"

For a moment I shrank back thinking, *how could he be so…what? Heartless to a poor pregnant mother with her children in such desperation!* But looking back, I now know that what he did was the kind deathblow to a pity-party waiting to happen that had the potential to plunge me into defeat. Through that—what I thought—cruel slap, I gave up on feeling sorry for myself and pressed into a realm of courage and hope. I was sobered to get up and start searching and finding this God whom I claimed to believe in, yet who had been most elusive in my life lately.

What happened? I kept asking myself incredulously. How did I fall into this hopeless faith—what an oxymoron that was!

The truth was now dawning in my searching heart. Even though I read my Bible dutifully and even taught God's Word in Sunday school, assurance and faith in God's power remained a great big mystery.

When did I lose that vibrant hope that I possessed in the beginning of my new life in Christ? How could I forget the love that liberated me from my old fears and torments? How could I settle for less than the faith that filled me with anticipation and wonder? I got sidetracked, but where and when? Why did I change direction and then go on with this way of life, trying to be acceptable in the eyes of those whom I perceived as better than me…the "religious giants" who appeared to know God in a deeper way than I did? Trying to please them started me on a frustrating quest of trying to please everybody, which became a hopeless cycle of disappointing experiences in my relationships. Little by little, all joy and love were smothered by the rules for correct behavior. By attempting to emulate the man-made ideal of what a "good Christian" should look like, talk like, and walk like, I adopted a merciless standard by which I judged myself and others. That fault-finding attitude systematically replaced the wonderful freedom and goodwill that I found when I first met the Savior in my living room years before. Back then, everything was forgiven, my joy was boundless, and my future was bright in the sure hope that God was in control of every aspect of my life. Then, in the process of trying to do what I was led to believe was right, I seemingly lost it all.

How could the loss of joy be part of God's plan for me? I asked secretly so as to not offend my "tutors of righteousness."

Why would God separate me from the pain of my past for a season of glorious liberty just to later plunge me into another existence that was choking the happiness out of every waking moment? That did not make sense!

What happened? I searched now with urgent fervency. Did I exchange my liberty for something that I did not bargain for just to fit in with the crowd?

Now in hindsight, it is so clear what happened. It is nothing new to most of us who have been set free to live a new life just to be entangled again in a hideous old trap.

What trap? The trap that is so hard to recognize when it appears the first time, always in "sheep's clothing," parading around as the "true religion that really pleases God."

How can a trap parade around in sheep's clothing? Quite cleverly. You see, these traps are some of the religious leaders themselves who have a self-promoting agenda (Galatians 4:17). With an air of "I am holier than you" (Isaiah 65:5), they snub those who do not live up to their self-tailored favoritism.

I had the displeasure of experiencing how this type of rejection can cause a wrong zeal to rise in the heart of one who longs to be accepted into the "inner circle." Very few newcomers to religion know that it is better to remain an "outsider" of those circles that disseminate a worldview of separation in the name of their superiority. I remember being greatly impressed by the pathos of those who were teaching the doctrines of men with a religious jargon. It sounded as if they were uttering the oracles of God. There was no way to see where they were going, and I would have never guessed that they were leading their unsuspecting followers on a crash course.

Before you think these are representatives of the other religions of the world, let me make it plain. Within our Christian churches, fellowships, and even our families we may encounter those who are bent on controlling others at all costs. (Christ gave us an example of this spirit in Matthew 15:1–14.) If allowed to rule, such a spirit would take control, with overt or covert manipulations, and attempt to constrain everyone to an existence that has nothing to do with the life that God granted us in Christ.

But if I was truly free in Christ, then why would I allow myself to get sidetracked into bondage? Good question. Maybe because this kind of dogma seems like a welcoming arm around one's shoulder at first; it did not alarm me that I was urged to move in a direction against my better judgment. By the time I questioned where we were heading, those friendly arms turned out to be like a heavy yoke that I could not escape from under in my own strength.

What yoke am I talking about?

Legalism. One simple word but laden with sinister potential. It points to a state of being, characterized by an overly strict adherence to laws motivated by pride and fear. It indicates a toxic, injurious pattern of thinking that would steal, kill, and destroy all joy, love, and peace of those who allow such thoughts to rule their minds. This elitist ideology overrules the greatest calling, to "love God and love one another," with grave consequences.

And because I was not an exception to immaturity, I, too, fell from the exuberant first love for my Lord into the dugout of the control freaks. Before I could make an educated choice about with whom I was joining, I found myself in the middle of it: dress-code, hairstyle, child-rearing philosophies, perfectionism, and judgmental expectations of everything under heaven. The initial longing to be pleasing in God's sight was replaced quite unnoticeably and gradually with the quest to be acceptable in the sight of the better-than-me saints. In those trenches, love for God degenerates into superstitious reverence for the law. Such an attitude can pop up almost anywhere. I am not referring to the people of any church in particular. This is not a denominational phenomenon. This is the deeply rooted human predicament of trying to manipulate others "for their own good."

Of course not all religious leaders are "holy controllers"; there are plenty of lay people who are driven to rule with the rod of iron in their microcosms, who are also unwittingly on a crusade to give Christianity a very bad reputation. Parading their opinions on how God does or does not do his work in the lives of his children, they pose as the experts about the "safety rules" on how to live for God, as if their approval was the precursor for God's favor…but only in their minds. The life of faith goes on in spite of them.

But how did we get into all this? Why am I going on and on about the woes of legalism? Because I fell for it, and, after being rescued, I want to sound a warning to all who are just coming into the wonderful provisions of God through Jesus Christ. We are to watch our steps so we do not stumble into a false belief system based on fear and pride.

The liberating truth is that in Christ we are set free from the old mindset! We are not expected to do one thing about being more acceptable or more loved by our heavenly Father! I did not realize this, or I forgot it, because of the teaching that God's love can be increased or decreased by our doings.

It cannot! God's love is unchangingly perfect!

However, before this experience, I did not learn this truth yet; instead, I was sold on the idea to have to work hard for God's favor, all in the name of "doing what is right" and unconcerned about *being right* in the intents of the heart.

Some say I should have known that conformity forced by fear tactics is not what God saved us for. But I didn't. Neither did I understand that it cannot be God's way to control others through the teaching of perpetual self-reproach. But since then, I came to realize that legalists do so in ignorance because they do not know any better. And that is the key to our restoration and freedom and, yes, forgiveness toward all who try to lord their authority over us!

One of my greatest hopes in writing this book is to help readers "get" the liberating truth about how to turn from the tragedy of religiosity to the triumphant faith in the love of God. Based on the understanding that none of us would fall prey to legalism if we knew better, we can lovingly extend a hand to those who are ready to be lifted out of the trenches of manipulative dogmas. And because experience is the grand tutor and a helpful deterrent, the lesson seldom needs repeating.

To be fair and for the sake of balance, let me point out another issue that should be considered here, or to use the same analogy, there is a ditch on the opposite side of the highway. Some readers might recognize this place from experience. Those who feel a bit smug right now for not being a legalist may be able to relate to the other sort of subjugation better. It is the pretext of liberalism, where anything goes in the "name of Jesus." Some of the members of these ranks may possibly be ex-legalists who overreacted to the straightjacket lifestyle on that side of the road and now will have nothing to do with any kinds of restrictions. Clearly, this is a risky attitude too, with major problems, not freedoms ahead. Sometimes believers fall for this kind of "easy believism," because it seems less stressful to live in denial than to deny the self that drives one's life into all sorts of mischief.

Most of us know what the dead-end streets of presumptions look like. What very few of us understand though is that only with divine help can we retrace our steps from those places of "religion gone wrong." And unless the desire for the balanced walk is developed to be stronger than the gravity of self-righteousness and fear, the inner ability to hear the call of freedom remains dormant. Why? Because of our deep-seated reluctance to pay attention to God, most of us would rather stay in the familiar circles... listening to the collective wisdom of those around us, seemingly content with a comatose subsistence filled with mediocre pleasures.

Alas, the lawless delight in feeling much better on that side of the road, completely blind to the fact that they are just as out of balance as their legalistic opponents. Comically, both sides call each other "hypocrites," and rightly so.

If anyone would try to point out the flaw in

the doctrine of "God is love, so I can do whatever I want!" such a brave soul might as well prepare to hear the passionate rebuffs from the proudly free spirited, such as: "Don't give me this 'my body is a temple' stuff…I don't need anybody to tell me what to do! I can quit anytime, and I'll do it when I feel like it. Just get off my back, you religious fanatic!"

Recently, a young person of the above persuasion left this world way too soon due to mixing substances that created a deadly overdose in his body. His last words betrayed his ruinous philosophy. He explained to his concerned friends that God had a great purpose for his life; therefore he was free and invincible until he had fulfilled that purpose. He took his liberty to a heartrending extreme when he put his trust in that erroneous belief just before going off to Bible college. What a tragic outcome caused by misinformation!

Let us pay attention—there are some teachings just as bad or worse as the legalist's! It is of utmost importance to understand, and to teach by example, that true freedom is always balanced by inspired responsibility.

When lacking the experiential knowledge of the Holy One, all of us are prone to accept and revert to different forms of the old knowledge of good and evil—the very thing Christ came to set us free from! The choices are presented to all of us daily: either the fruit of "good and evil" or the fruit from the "tree of life." The Son of God brought to us the balanced, fresh revelation of the Father's love for his children. Those who believe Christ and partake of his words will be well nourished and thriving in joyous relationship with God, as Father.

The teachings of the fear-peddlers are easily recognized and rejected by those who have "tasted and have seen that the Lord is good." Someone who knows from experience how it feels to hear from God will not fall for the discordant voices of the gods made in man's image.

For an example, which voice would you recognize as God's: the one that reminds you of the everlasting arms of love around you, coupled with the corresponding feelings of being cherished and protected, or would you rather believe the familiar voices that remind you of your list of wrongdoings, coupled with the feelings of hopelessness and the need to strive harder for favors? Is the voice of God the one that inspires you to understand and then enables you to forgive, or is it the one that entices you to judge and then compels you to play the blame game that leaves you with the sickening feelings of being right about withholding mercy from that "undeserving brute"?

Those who hear from God are always uplifted, never downtrodden. God's voice offers delicious newness of joy, and would never attempt to force-feed you with stale old dogmas.

None of us should accept the bitter fruit of self-righteousness or the other extreme, the nauseatingly sweetened "easy believism" served up from the ditches of false doctrines!

Yet, without discernment, many fall to one side or the other because, all too often, there are not enough living examples who would point new believers to God's orchard of living joy to partake of. For lack of this understanding, many new believers slip into the "sin/guilt/shame ditch" by trying to appease a capricious god (made in the likeness of nitpicky man), while others may descend, quite willingly, into the other ditch, where they can continue to slumber in complacency and denial, in the arms of their "sugar daddy god."

As much as I do not like to admit this, and in spite of how repugnant legalism smelled and tasted, I bought into the idea that the displeasure I was feeling—while imbibing the doctrines of fear and pride—was part of God's justice. This ill logic suggested that I had to go through a "cleansing process" to deal with my past, which in turn trapped me in a prideful deception that "I was suffering for Jesus." With time, this fallacious teaching took over to such an extent that the first love for my Lord gradually became just a faint memory. I spent most of my days in frustrated and disappointed struggles with myself, my family, and others. None of us measured up. The harder we tried, the worse it felt. But I did not dare turn away from trying even harder, because that kind of reaction was marked as "denying the Lord…fire and brimstone on you!" The only way to cope in that excruciating state of being was to become numb. However, that was not my personality. I kept fighting the losing battle, which is, as you can imagine, an exhausting lifestyle.

That is why the sermon that previous Sunday was so unsettling yet intriguing. The message got my attention, it stirred me up. Somehow it reminded me of a better God than what I had bought into. I was thoroughly dissatisfied with the choice between sleep-walking and a fake life, but I did not know that there was a better option—God's.

Now, in this overwhelming desperation, I needed to find this better God. The one with rationed favor was losing altitude over me with great velocity. I wanted out. I wanted out of believing in the man-dictated-standardized-heavenly "task master."

I needed to find the God of mercy, the God

of miraculous power, the God who promised that "All things work together for good..." (Romans 8:28, NKJV), not only for the "better" believers but for me, too!

Desperately and willingly, I gave up on the idea to earn God's benevolence. I fervently sought his mercy as undeserving as I was. There was no time to earn brownie points now. I needed to run back to the God and Savior I first came to believe in...the one who had hope for me.

I rejected my wretchedness in God's eyes and asked with everything in me from the depth of my heart: God, show me how this hopelessness can work out for our good!

...To Reveal...

Finally, the door of the intensive care opened to a large room with many beds. Every bed was occupied by a child in grave condition. The only way I could bear this moment was by focusing on my little one who lay there like a rag doll with wires and tubes hanging from each side. He just stared ahead with those strange eyes and did not respond to anything. No amount of coaxing moved him. We tried gently at first to make him react to something, anything! I touched his arm, face, hair, legs, but nothing seemed to register. Our voices were not reaching him. *Is he on something? Maybe he is drugged,* I thought.

The nurse spoke with sympathy about the recovery that could take weeks or months. Then she spoke about patience. She, too, understood that we could not reply to her predictions. We were just trying to stay afloat at this sight. Finally, she encouraged me to hold him if I wanted to.

"With the wires and all?" I asked.

"Yes, you can rock him in the chair here," she replied gently.

Oh how the rush of almost overwhelming excitement came over me! With shaking hands we grabbed him and, with some struggle, my husband placed him on my very short lap. (Remember, my pregnant belly.)

Finally, I could hold him, and I did not ever want to let go of him—ever. I wanted to soak him in my love, to pour life into him with every kiss. Oh, how sweet he smelled, how wonderful his silky skin felt on mine.

"Oh, God! Lord! Work it out for good! Please, Lord…please…" I repeated with every sway of the rocking-chair.

There was such compassion on every face looking at us from the other beds. Parents with sorrow over their little ones somehow took a break by observing us, the newcomers to this world of unashamed clinging to one another.

On one side was a desperately ill child with mother and father at her side, holding hands, smiling at us encouragingly. The mother stepped over and asked what happened. My husband said the bare minimum, trying not to be rude. But they understood. They seemed to know where we were at. She volunteered to talk to us without expecting us to respond. It turned out as they shared their story that they have been in this place for years. They have been in and out of needing emergency care for their daughter. This was now part of their lives. As I listened to their words, my face was turned toward my boy.

I could not bear the thought of looking at such desperation. Years! I shivered at the thought. How could they go on like this?

As if the woman heard my thoughts, she told us how this changed their whole life and how through this endless ordeal, with no improvement in sight, they have found a faith in God that is unshakable and real.

At this, I could not help but look up at the source of these unbelievable words. The mother's face was bright and truthful, and so was her husband's. He assured us that after a while it stops hurting, and then it just becomes part of life to have to come here and hope for the best. They were thankful!

Their words were astonishing, but I could not accept them. *No! Not for us!* My heart cried in desperation. *Please God! Not this! Please not this!*

On the other side of us was an infant dressed in colorful clothing. She was a rather strange sight in a place like this. The nurse told us she never left the hospital since her birth. She had a long way to go, but there was hope. The mom held her little one's tiny hand and seemed almost comfortable. She talked softly to her child as if everything was just as it should be.

No! I turned my eyes away. *No! God! Have mercy…I can't…please get us out of here…please! God, have mercy!*

The pain was almost unbearable to look at.

My unborn was stirring and pushing on the inside, almost as if feeling my pain, too. *Oh, God, have mercy on us all!* I pleaded. *Get us out of here, I beg you! Please have mercy. I see that the other families seem to be okay with this. God, forgive me for not wanting to talk to them. God, help me to understand. Bless them, yes, bless them all. Just get us out of here!*

The visitation was soon over. We had to leave and once again agonized about trusting our son to others. We so wanted to be with him.

It was time to check into the cheerfully decorated Ronald McDonald House where we were to reside however long it took until his recovery.

Because it was the Christmas season, bells, lights, pictures, and all were trying to bring the movement of the outside world into ours. There was a huge dinner for the residents arranged around a big table. A group was caroling, and between the songs we sat in somber silence. The lady in charge tried to keep conversations going, but every attempt came to an abrupt halt. Trying to lighten me up, she asked in a joking fashion, "Did you have a rough day at the office?" I stared at her in disbelief.

Not wanting to hurt her feelings, I just shook my head. She chirped on, kindly mothering me, "Honey, you need to eat. Come on, think of this one" pointing to my middle. "You need to get a grip and eat so you can go on."

My husband came to my rescue, "Thank you," he said, "she will be all right. Just give us a moment." He led me to a seat and served me a huge plate of food. I could not bear the thought of chewing and swallowing—not even one bite. I remember wondering what would happen to my unborn child if I could not eat.

The kind volunteers sang one song after another while I sat and stared at the tablecloth. Everything seemed unbearably unreal. "I can't do this," I whispered to my husband. "I have to go to the room."

"But you must eat, sweetie," he whispered encouragingly.

"I can't. I'm sorry. I have to go now!"

There was another kind of hunger in me...a completely new, starving kind. I needed to get alone with my God. I needed answers. I had to get to God somehow or I would cease to exist.

In the room, I reached for my bag and started unpacking. But after the first few items, I fell to my knees at the bed and begged, "God! I can't go on! I can't deal with this!"

As if it were yesterday, I remember the astonishment as I watched a yellow slip of paper float out of my Bible.

The outline! There it is! It appeared like a lifeline, and I grabbed it with a mixture of disbelief and amazement. Like a starving one, I hungrily pored over the words that I scribbled onto the blank spaces on Sunday: "Sometimes God allows hopeless situations to reveal his true character and miraculous power."

Suddenly I knew without a shadow of a doubt that God himself was talking to me. No, I did not hear voices, yet it was completely audible to a part of me that I had not given attention to before. Speaking out loud, I answered eagerly, "Okay, got it! Yes, my Lord! I understand. What am I to do now?"

The verse came to my mind again. "All things work together for good…" What is the rest of it? I searched feverishly in my Bible. Found it! Romans 8:28. I held my breath in dismay as I read the words: "…to them that love God, to them who are called according to His purpose" (NKJV). I stared at those words for a long time.

In God's light there was no denying the horrifying truth. I knew there was no hiding it, there was no white-washing it, and there was no escaping it. My love for God was at best a questionable emotion, a mental consent that I should love him out of duty. The reality of that first love was long forgotten in my indoctrinated heart, like the sweetness of a honeymoon is remembered with a disillusioned chuckle after years of growing apart.

But now...I tried to get back there, but could not figure out how?

"Oh God! I want to love you! But I don't... at least not like I should. I am so sorry! Have mercy on me! Make me love you! Make me love you more!" I whispered with my heart pounding in my throat.

Like a movie in reverse, I was ushered backwards in time. I recognized defining moments in chronological order—times when I turned from patience to anger, from mercy to judgment, from faith to doubt, from dependence on God to presumption, from submission to control, from humility to pride, from love to hate.

So that's how it happened! It was a sobering and enlightening journey. Now I had to backtrack...from the reactive thought-processes of my mind I had to find the path back to my heart. When I finally arrived at the end of those torturous memories, there I found a place of joyful, childlike trust.

I had forgotten this place of sparkling hope in an invisible yet good God who loved me more than I could comprehend. Then I remembered that I did love God...once! I did! I just exchanged his love for the acceptance into a circle of people I wanted to belong to.

I took a long look at the past with its disappointed hopes and wasted efforts and turned my back on it all.

"Oh, God! Take me back! Take me back to Jesus, my loving Lord! I'm coming back!"

I could not have explained it then, but somehow I sensed a change in direction; at that moment I turned from the tragedy of make-believe religion to a triumphant faith in God.

As if I was coming back to life, I became aware of a maddening thirst for water. I drank from a bottle for a long time. The Bible lay on the bed calling me; I did what I taught others not to do—I opened it up at random. This religious strategy, of not reading the Bible in a disorderly fashion, was not my own idea. I was just parroting what I heard from the "holier ones." It felt good to shake off that straightjacket-like teaching.

The book opened up, and again that inaudible yet powerful voice spoke to me as clearly as if someone was right next to me reading it:

"Sanctify yourselves for tomorrow morning the Lord will do a miracle." (Joshua 3:5, NKJV).

To me, this was an absolute unshakable precise instruction from God himself. Without a hint of questioning his promise, I took it as information about God's plan of action. And even though it did not happen yet, I knew what the miracle was going to be.

With dizzy joy, I tried to get up and get the news to my husband. I met him at the door as he was walking into the room. To his bewilderment he found me in euphoria trying to explain to him what just happened.

Yes! I was sure that God's promise was as good as if it had already happened. In other words, I felt certain that my hope was waiting to happen; we just did not catch up with tomorrow yet.

Without a shadow of a doubt, I was so sure... and my husband was so sorry. His face betrayed the inner struggle as he was trying to hide his doubts from me. He did not want to take my joy away with his skepticism. He was hoping that I might go and eat now that I felt better. But food was the furthest thing from my mind. I hungered for my husband's partnership more than physical nourishment. I desired to draw him into this place of miraculous faith to partake of.

After sharing with him God's message to me

step by step, he felt some hope rise, but he quickly squelched it. He did not want me to be disappointed in case…But I asked him desperately to "please believe with me."

He gave me a long look with those big blue eyes. I saw a tear forming and then I heard his choked up voice. "All right."

We knelt and prayed with an agreement that was unusual for us. He prayed with a willingness that originated in his desperate need to have his doubts overruled by a good and merciful God. I did not have to tell him what to ask for.

Did our prayer and faith qualify? Well, that is all we had. We were more than willing to be rescued from a life of secondhand faith. At this point, the half-hearted understanding of God's words became unacceptable to us. We searched the Bible with anticipation.

Now I was earnestly seeking to find what the word "sanctify" really meant. I was eager to follow God's directions with understanding. He said to sanctify ourselves, but what did that really mean to us? My husband explained that it had something to do with cleansing and being committed, but he was not sure.

"Cleansing what?" I wondered. As I mused over this question, my eyes kept returning to the sign on the table.

"Cleaning Instructions" it read in bold writing. The step-by-step directions informed the occupants what to do before vacating the room. To my surprise I identified these as our instructions to move into an action of faith. Our commitment to believe God, instead of what we heard from the doctors, wanted to be expressed. The future that our fears tried to project ahead of us was thoroughly rejected and replaced with the vibrant hope of a miracle. In order to line up with God's promise, this seemingly senseless activity became our next step to follow. I really wanted to believe God's Word; therefore the only actions I could think of were: stop unpacking and follow the rules of cleaning the room before we leave the Ronald McDonald House the next morning.

"But it is night time! We have just arrived! We didn't make anything dirty yet! Why clean now?"

My husband's reluctance soon faded as he watched me wiping the window sills with meticulous care and reverence. This action was not to make deals with God. I did not do it to appease a task master. I did not seek to deserve anything. For the first time in my life, I understood that the living God, who led me into this expression of hope, did not do so to obligate me for some kind of exchange. God inspired me to this action to bring me out of apathy and resignation so that our focus would not be on what we were told to expect for our son. We were offered a new mindset that trusted God's almighty power, being convinced of divine involvement through clear communication. That is how far my faith extended at this point of my life. And believe me, it was a great improvement.

When God gave those words to call us to sanctification, he called us to faith in him, not to a ritualistic display of self-effort to see if we deserved his mercy.

God does not make contracts like, "If you do this, I'll do that," which are the dealings suggested by the religious leaders in their misguided lust for control.

God loves us!

In that light, my efforts to earn God's goodwill seemed totally unnecessary…almost an offense against his character…to act as if God waited on me to perform before he would start working things out "for good."

I was sure by now that God saw what was in my heart. The Omniscient, the One who knows all things, knew what was being uncovered and beginning to bud below the rubble of legalism, even before I had a clue.

By following those instructions to clean our

room, I was not trying to earn anything, to prove my submission, or to obligate God.

I cleaned because that was the action that kept me moving by faith in his promise. I took it seriously because this was the challenge of my life...of believing and acting and walking out what I trusted God to do. If he was to miraculously heal my child, I was to walk accordingly now—not after it was done, but before, during, and after the manifestation of his promise. This was new territory to us.

. . . *His True Character* . . .

There he was, vacuuming the rug in the middle of the night; there I was, scrubbing the clean shower wall—both acting as if our lives depended on it.

Finally, my husband had had enough, and he declared the place "clean." The morning was still hours away.

What are we going to do until sunrise?

The beds were made, every wrinkle straightened out. We looked at each other, and then my husband realized what I needed most. He took me by the hand and knelt with me to speak to God one more time, desperately pleading, yet believing that we would not be disappointed in our faith, as undeserving as we were. He spoke as a child to a good daddy without trying to make a deal with God.

Just when I felt like congratulating him for how he rose to the occasion in such an amazing way, he straightened up and said with a very uncharacteristic force in his voice: "And now we will go to bed and sleep!"

Before I could protest, he threw the covers back and literally fell asleep on the spot.

But the beds were already made! If we sleep in them, we have to wash all the sheets and remake the beds. That will cost precious time! I struggled for a while inwardly, but I had to admit my body was about to crumble if I did not at least put my feet up. As I listened to my husband's slow rhythmical breathing, my emotions were calmed.

Yes, he is right! I need to use this time to rest awhile. Carefully, I peeled the cover back on the other bed and lay there turned toward the window to catch the first sign of light. My body felt like lead, but my mind was still searching.

How could this happen to us? Why? Quickly, I realized that this was the wrong road…the wrong thoughts…the wrong focus.

Instead of dwelling on those thoughts, I pulled out that miraculous sheet of paper again. I reread the points of the sermon outline and then pondered the words in the Bible that promised a miracle in the morning…just a few hours away.

How is God going to do it? Is he healing our son right now? I wondered.

What is the Almighty doing right now? I

mused trying to picture God who gave me those instructions to get ready. My mind was kept steady by the words repeating over and over. *"All things work together for good to those..."*

I want to be one of "those." God, I want to love you! But I don't—not the way I think you deserve. Maybe after tomorrow morning I will have a reason to love you, God! Forgive me! I wish I could love you now! I wish I had it in me now! That love...the love I lost or exchanged? But for what...for the praise of people?...the people I so admired for loving you? How crazy this is! Lord, what happened to that love? Could you find it and give it back to me...that wonderful thankfulness for saving me...that feeling of finally being found by you, Lord? I reminisced sadly.

God! I long to see you, I whispered in my heart, but my mind intercepted the yearning with a negative wave of misgiving. *Well, I guess I can't do that.* I recalled the teaching that asserted that no one can see God and live.

Well then, let me hear your voice. But, of course, that could not work either. I was told that hearing voices was a sign of insanity, not godliness.

But then with what can I satisfy this aching desire?

Please God! Reveal yourself to me...the way you want to...just so that I know it is you!

The minutes dragged on, but no sleep came.

The streetlights shed enough light through the window so I could read. The sermon outline seemed like a news-clip from the future, as if handed to me to explain what happened and why and what the outcome would be. The encouragement of those words was coming to a very open heart now...a very needy and attentive heart. At this moment, I remembered what had stirred me on Sunday as I listened to the preacher. He was talking about life with Christ—not the hypocritical make-believe life of a man-made religion masquerading as Christianity. He spoke about a life full of joy and love in spite of circumstances. This was mind-boggling to me at first, but then a memory was stirred in me. I had a person like that in my life. In my early childhood, my grandmother was an example of that kind of faith, but I did not understand it then. I thought she was born that way...one of the lucky, one of the few who could stay calm and full of love when the world was going crazy around her. How would she be in a circumstance such as we were in at present? Her memory made me wonder, to recall, and to desire to be like that.

According to what the preacher said, with God even that was possible. Not only possible, but God is actually calling us to that kind of life. Calling us!

"The verse!" I exclaimed.

"All things work together for good to those who love God and are called according to his purpose."

Called! Called for what?

"For his purpose."

What is God's purpose for me? I searched intently. I had some ideas about my purpose, such as raising my children right, getting my husband "with it," trying to be nice to others, and so on. But what was God's purpose for my life?

Could God's purpose be different from mine?

Again, I noticed with dismay that God was not even part of my plan. Of course to others, I would have given the answer to the question about our purpose as human beings. My Sunday school answer was: "To glorify God and enjoy him forever."

But God and I knew that this was just parroting words without any reality. It was not my life's true statement, but today I was making progress. At least by now I was not trying to fool myself or God. I knew he knew.

So what if God had a call on my life, and I did not even know about it? Not because he hid it from me, but because I never bothered to even think past my agenda?

With childlike sincerity I asked, "God! Are you calling me for something? What is your purpose for my life?"

As if I was wrapped in a cocoon of all-consuming peace with God, I heard a gentle voice in that solitude.

"Do you love me?"

Without any alarm I felt my response rise to God.

"I want to, Lord! I really do! You know that!"

My answer came from my heart, not my head…truly more from the direction of my chest.

"Seek my face!" God whispered.

"But I do not want to die!" I whispered back into that realm that I had just realized existed.

"Seek my face!" God persisted.

"I will…but what does that mean? All I see is the darkness behind my eyelids…"

"I have loved you with an everlasting love." I heard in reply.

I knew this was a verse in the Bible. This caused great joy to bubble up in me.

Then I thought, maybe this is what that older woman was talking about when she asserted once in my hearing, "The Lord told me today about such and such…" I was convinced that only the very good saints heard from God himself. In my estimation, I was totally and permanently disqualified, according to what I heard and knew myself to be. My past life was a series of bad choices and blunders; I was sure that sealed my future forever. It was an old chronic thinking pattern, which barred me from ever amounting to anything for God.

At that moment, in the deepest agony and the highest revelation of my life, this mindset was recognized as lacking the most important ingredient: genuine love for God.

I was alone. Nobody could be where I was at this moment. I felt so exposed, naked, yet without the urge to cover up to hide what I turned out to be in the sight of God. Finally, at last, I was undeniably who I was in the all-knowing eyes of God. I found myself in the presence of divine goodwill; and instead of cowering in shame, I felt somehow welcomed. God met me where no one else could enter.

If this was real, I mused, how very good my God is...how kind and merciful, how forgiving and understanding, how willing to help me, how wonderfully gentle and patient.

Again that eye in me looked upward with thankful appreciation at these thoughts and then: a most beautiful sight!

No, not a picture or a vision, yet an undeniable encounter. The presence of overwhelming love looked back at me.

Like the fragrance of a rose, the gentleness of a dove, yet the power of a mighty waterfall, sparkling glory flooded my darkness—and even these words are but a feeble attempt to describe someone beyond words.

Instantly, my tears started flowing, quietly and gently soaking many tissues. There was no stopping them now. Even my fear of messing up the pillow was swept away. I basked and rested in this wonderful timeless moment.

I felt benign warmth on my face as I wept and wept.

How lovely, how very lovely you are! I kept looking upward for a glimpse to see if God was still there and then cried quietly in a most comforting embrace.

Yes…embrace.

After a while there was a big need for more tissues and, to my amazement, going to get a roll of toilet paper did not break up this precious union. I could say that I fell in love with my Lord, but that expression would not do justice to what actually happened. It was more that in his presence I rose up to enter into God's love.

And here comes the most mind-boggling part: in this place it did not matter what happened with me. It did not even matter what would happen in the morning.

From this new place, the life I had lived up to now was left behind with all its fears, demands, plans, and hopes. But, most importantly, the "love-lessness" was left behind also.

A resurrection to love again! That is what it was like. Through this awakening to a new appreciation for the spoken Word of God, at last I understood that truly those words are alive! God speaks through the written Word; and in addition to the reading of the Word, we are enabled to hear God's voice with the inner ear of our heart. All of us can…the moment we pay attention!

I noticed a never before experienced freedom in my chest after that long cry. I found myself breathing in and out as if satisfying a thirst for air after being confined in a tight place for a long time. An unprecedented joy was taking over. I had an urge to hug my Lord. God was so close, reassuring me that he would never leave me. How I cherish that revelation.

This encounter with God changed my life. Even before his promise would be fulfilled, which I hoped would give me reason to love him in return for doing me a favor; I knew that my love for God was real. Somehow I was led to a place of uncomplicated, childlike trust. Or did I just simply turn toward God's call? One thing I was sure of, I knew I could never go back to that awful place of trying to earn favors from that make-believe god who was created in the attitudes and controlling minds of the past. I noticed with great relief that my God set me free from the works of fear and guilt.

How I thanked him! I was changed!

I knew our future would be different. I could now love again. My husband and children were going to be free, too, because I was not going to control them by my fears of not measuring up.

Was it lack of food, lack of sleep, or all of it together? I felt a dizzy joy all over me. I could hardly wait for my husband to wake up. I wanted to tell him that I loved him. This I have not done for some time because I did not want him to assume that his halfhearted efforts at being the spiritual leader were enough.

I withheld love and affection because I did not want to make him relax any further into disinterest and his quiet rebellion against God. At least, that was my reasoning then. It was so clear now. We were called to live in God's love. Not in the approval of those we thought better than we were. I knew I was free, and I wanted to set my husband and my children free from that old zeal to please others rather than our beloved Lord.

Oh, how I thanked God for the hope of being able to love my children again with that motherlove that I allowed to be suppressed by fear.

I scribbled on the yellow outline paper: "I really love you!"...and then let the tears erupt again. I knew the statement was true at last. I did love God and understood his call to freedom. The freedom in Christ to love God and one another with and within his perfect love!

. . . And His Power

The quiet of the night gave way slowly; the new morning came at last with breathtaking excitement. Under our window the traffic started with the usual hustle, but to me this was more than just another day. This was a day of hope…a day with a promise…a new day, not like yesterday or tomorrow!

My tired husband did not know what to think anymore…a wife so stirred up and filled with surprising contradiction…with a puffed up face from hours of crying…exulting in joyful anticipation…hugging and saying lovely words about freedom…tearing the sheets off the beds with vigor (to complete the cleaning instructions)…performing the final touches of our "sanctification" with singing. He just shook his head and went along with me to hope.

Before we left the room with our belongings, he tried one last time: "Why don't we just leave our stuff in here until after the morning visit?

But I pleaded, "Remember what God promised? Let's go all the way! Let's do everything as if it happened already! Please, let's believe together!"

The encouragement got through to him once again. He held me in a tender embrace as we prayed, preparing us for our miracle. I held my breath as I heard his voice rise once again to faith for the impossible.

On our way to the intensive care unit, we were quiet. Suddenly the eagerness to get there on time gave way to mixed emotions.

What will happen? How is God going to do it? What was waiting beyond those closed doors? What will happen when we walk through them? Will our boy just sit up and say "Hi," and we will simply take him home? What will we say?

As we waited outside for the clock to tick into position, we tried to peek through the spaces where the door panels met.

We could see slivers of the world inside the intensive care, but our little one was not in view. *Maybe he got better overnight and was taken to another location, a regular room with toys.* My mind was trying to come up with all kinds of combinations about this great hope in my heart.

But there was a desperate "what if" also clamoring for attention at my side. Remember, that dark hole representing hopelessness that was so close to me just the day before? Now that black abyss was far removed, yet not completely out of sight.

My husband and I tried to avoid too many words. We were focusing, mentally preparing for what was ahead.

I was becoming reverently aware of the power of words. One way or another, spoken words have the power of maintaining or destroying hope. We were careful, with a deep understanding of our responsibility of using our tongue for allowing only the language that was in alignment with our faith in God. Instinctively we refused to speak the terminology of foreboding expectations. I had never known that I could pick and chose my thoughts and words by willing focus. How promising this understanding was at this moment.

From the beginning God always spoke with a clear intent for his Word to perform what he sent it for into every situation. Shouldn't we also take our words seriously, lining up intent with the content of our conversations?

As we waited silently in the corridor, I became aware of a little song playing in my mind over and over. I learned it from my mentor friend who put these words to a happy tune to teach children how to greet a new day with the right attitude.

This is the day that the Lord has made. Not like tomorrow or yesterday. He made this day in a special way. So let us all sing and be glad!

Presently, these words opened up a revelation before me. This day was made by God! This day was already done in God's realm! God has willed this day to bring miraculous healing to our boy. It is done! And nobody can mess it up!

Where did this assurance come from? Where did this extra dose of confidence flow from? These were new thoughts, quite opposite from my regular thought patterns.

I realized with thankful amazement that I had changed, even in the way I used my mind. Scripture after Scripture that I had memorized now came back and crowded out my old ways of reasoning. The pride-fear-guilt-shame-hopelessness cycle was replaced by revelations of what those Scriptures really meant in a practical way to us now.

Then the Lord's Prayer captured my attention with a fresh revelation of its beauty and power. Prior to this moment, I could rattle it off with one breath without the slightest hint or desire for deeper comprehension or application; and I had taught my children to do likewise. Did they understand what they were saying? It did not matter as long as they could repeat it flawlessly.

But today...this day...these words became miraculously precious!

"Our Father in Heaven"...beloved Daddy...here we are, this is your day!

"Hallowed be Your Name"...how we love you for who you really are...it is so good to know that you are our loving Father!

"Your Kingdom come"...whatever you prepared in heaven for today is what we want more than anything.

"Your will be done"...please do everything your way, just exactly how you planned it and help us here on earth to move along with you through it all.

"On earth as it is in Heaven"...we long to have heaven on earth today...to see your plan fulfilled in our lives...for you alone are our loving Father and King...we desire to live with you all the way every day.

"Give us this day our daily bread"...*wow!* I thought, *Father, I haven't eaten now for a day and had no feelings of hunger...You sustained me...I did not lack anything. Thank you!*

The breakfast trays were rattling toward us. We had to step aside to let them be pushed through the door. Hungrily, we looked into the room in the direction of where we left our boy the night before. Just a glimpse! How is he? Is he waiting for us?

His bed was visible just for a moment as the panels closed before our faces. He seemed asleep, propped up with those wires and tubes still attached. My heart wanted to sink. I was careful not to look into my husband's eyes. But his hopeful voice reached me comfortingly: "Oh, good! He is still sleeping."

That's right! I followed gladly after his observation: it is good! Our boy is still sleeping, and it is good. How thankful I was for my husband's interpretation of that sight. Soon after that we were finally allowed to enter. The nurse was busy around him. As we slowly tiptoed over to his bed, I searched for some signs of change in his condition.

"How is he doing?" we whispered.

"Oh, he is catching up on some sleep," she chirped almost boisterously as she bustled around his placid body.

"Is he on something?" we probed. "He is not waking up."

"No, no! He didn't get anything. We are going to do some tests today, and then we will see. Right now he is just resting." she informed us kindly.

"Well," we hesitated for a long moment, "we are taking him home today."

The nurse stopped and froze in her movement. She stared at us incredulously.

"We believe God healed him."

She sighed and came closer. "Oh, honey. I believe in miracles, too, but he will have to show some signs, you know."

"Like what?" I asked, ready to take mental notes.

"Well, like..." she looked at the breakfast tray, "like eating on his own, you know...recognize you two, get up and walk over to you. But right now he is not even able to focus."

"What do you mean?" my question slipped out while I was trying to get rid of the tightness in my throat.

She hesitated for a moment. "His eyes..." her words were coming haltingly, then she quickly excused herself. "Let me get the doctor. He will explain to you what you need to know."

While the nurse was away, we tried to wake up our sleeping baby, stroking his feet first, then his legs, gently touching every precious limb. His face was very peaceful...almost too peaceful. We whispered to him encouraging words about going home.

As we were unsuccessful to get him to react to us, I noticed my words turning toward God to get a response from Him.

"Father, look! What is going on? Is he still tired? What should we do, Lord? What are we to do now?"

This was a secret conversation; these words were whispered in the room, but toward heaven, they were loud cries of pleading. I gazed at our little one; his eyes were still closed, but he did stir.

"Good morning," said the doctor.

There were several people in white coats surrounding us. Carefully avoiding eye-contact, we blurted out words that seemed almost ridiculous even to us: "We are taking him home. We believe he is okay now. We prayed, and…"

The answer came back to us like a tidal wave against our little ripples.

"We cannot release him yet, but as soon as he is showing improvement, we will assess the time for you to…"

"It is today! We know it is today!"

"Mr. and Mrs. Hinton, right?" The man in charge looked up from his chart. "Your child will have to go through some tests today, and after that we can give you an approximate date. He will have to go through rehab. This is standard…"

"Yes, but this is different," I pleaded. "He is healed!"

A female voice spoke up: "Mr. and Mrs. Hinton,

your child was near death. Give it some time. He has a good chance."

There were more white coats moving toward us. "We cannot release him in this condition!" one of them said firmly.

"What condition does he have to be in?" I heard myself asking.

"He will have to be able to focus, stand up, recognize objects...and you, Mrs. Hinton. He will have to show signs of restoration to his nervous system...you know...eat, walk, and so on."

"All right!" I heard my voice again. "We will just wait here with him until he is ready."

"All right," replied the doctor. "I'm glad you understand."

I turned to my boy and said to him: "Did you hear that, sweetie? You are going to have to get up and show them. C'mon, let's go home."

He was still in a light slumber. My hands stroked his hair and his velvety skin. He was like a little cherub in a place of tranquility, so content, a picture of beauty...except those wires! "When will they get those things off?" I directed the question upward to my God.

Then I looked around to make sure I was not seen talking into the air. To my surprise, some of the people were still around our bed. Amazingly, it did not bother me if they thought I was crazy or a fanatic.

When I looked back at my son, his eyes were open. It appeared as if the darkness, caused by his dilated pupil, was receding as he blinked several times, turning his head from side to side. I looked intently, following his movements. There was something strange again about his eyes. When his head came to a halt, he just stared ahead.

God! My Lord, his eyes!" I searched for that inner eye in me to get a glimpse of my hope.

Lord, help his eyes to focus. Groaning and begging, I kept looking upward.

Where was that excitement we had earlier? It turned into a fiery struggle against discouragement.

He sneezed and coughed a little, contorting his face into a funny expression. A wave of joy swept over us; it reminded us of his sweet little antics.

This gave me an idea. Winnie the Pooh, his favorite friend! He will want to focus on that!

I pulled the toy out of my bag, as if I had found the "key player" in our hope. When he opened his eyes again, there Winnie the Pooh was, looking at him with that familiar greeting for his best friend.

We had played this before. The stuffed friend was always able to get him up in the morning. However, there was a difference today. The animator was becoming one with the puppet. There was urgency and a hint of desperation in Winnie's voice. Nevertheless, the bear still remembered the favorite dance and hop that brought out that belly laughter every time.

"Good morning!" Winnie the Pooh said slowly. "What are you still doing in bed? Let's go and play! C'mon, King Richard, let's go!"

Lord, help! God! the bear's animator cried inside. *Please, Lord! I can't hold on too much longer.*

Without any warning or great show, our boy turned his head toward his bear.

My heart wanted to leap out.

"Rich!" I cried. "Look!"

Deliriously happy, we were watching his eyes rest on the stuffed toy. And…his pupils!

His eyes got the blue back! His sparkling blue eyes were back…however, as we moved closer to see, we were surprised again. Now what? The pupils were so tiny that they looked strange again, but in a much better way! What does this mean now? - we wondered.

"Ma'am," my husband called to the nurse. "Look! His eyes are all right!"

The nurse came and said cautiously: "Oh, that's right. Let's see, does he follow the object?"

I moved Winnie to the side slowly. His precious eyes followed!

Encouraged and overwhelmed with joy, Pooh bear started to dance and hop around, celebrating every move of his little friend.

Oh, God. Thank you! Thank you with all my heart! Oh, Lord. Yes! Let's keep going.

"What else?" I addressed the nurse without taking my eyes off of our son.

"What else must he do?" my husband's excited voice demanded.

"Well," the nurse's hesitating voice faded, and then we heard the feet of others coming toward us. But we did not look. We were focusing on our boy, the most marvelous sight in the entire world.

"Well, how about that!"

"This is a different child here."

There was a mixture of voices and good-natured cheers as some of the wires were peeled off.

"See if he can stand."

"Okay!" we eagerly obeyed the instructions.

My husband grabbed him and stood him up on the bed, while Winnie the Pooh kept his eyes entertained.

He stood, a little wobbly, but he stood!

"Look at that!" someone called out.

"Okay, now walk over here. Come to Momma!" I pleaded with torrents of tears running down my face. "Look, Winnie is waiting."

"C'mon, little Richie!" his daddy called, trying

to empower him with the strength in his voice. It worked!

He stretched out his arms and walked to us at the end of the bed among happy shouts bursting forth from everyone.

Were there any dry eyes? I do not know. My hardest chore was to keep my composure…whatever was left in me.

"What else? What else?" we asked eagerly.

"How about food? Try some food. See if he can hold it down," the suggestion came.

A tray of food materialized, and with trembling hands I put the straw in his favorite juice. "He likes this!" I assured everybody. The crowd was growing around us.

As he started sucking on the straw, we broke out in jubilation. The moment he finished a few sips the whole juice came back up—all over my arm. The dread was kicked right out of my mind. I refused to be bullied around by the fear that this was of any consequence whatsoever.

"Oh, this was just a little too cold. Please, give him something warm like oatmeal or grits." With my voice calm, almost as if this was expected and now we were ready for the real proof of his restoration.

Looking back now, it was just as miraculous that these wonderful people played along. They brought some warm mushy stuff. It smelled good. We watched him eat about three bites as I silently prayed for every spoon full: *Oh Lord, let it stay in his stomach and nourish him—please!* And it did!

He ate the food thoughtfully, looking at all the faces following his movements…opening our mouths with him as he opened his and rejoicing with every swallow.

When he had enough he turned to his friend Winnie again.

My arms were shaking so hard, but I would not dare let go of him.

"Please, undo the wires. He is ready!" I whispered, blinking away my tears.

My husband's humble yet uncompromising instructions soothed my emotions as he asked for his release.

A strong voice, demanding respect superseded all others by declaring: "This is one of those unexplainable phenomena!"

There was a moment of silence at these words. I was stunned and speechless at this statement. What did he mean? What does that mean to us? Will they let him go? Just as fear tried to creep in on me, I heard a familiar voice…a strong, determined, gloriously changed, yet still recognizable voice.

"This is a miracle of God! That's what it is!"

said my miraculously changed husband, reverently but firmly. With deep respect I looked at him in wholehearted agreement.

There were other responses to this statement, even to this day. Some were incredulous, some in full agreement, joyously acknowledging that they had witnessed something wonderful.

The wires were coming off his body, and my excitement was growing above what I could handle. A kind of hysteria was trying to take over, but someone in the group around us, quite unexpectedly, helped me out with his words.

The voice got my attention suddenly. It came from my right side, almost as if from the direction of the shoes. Maybe because that is where I kept staring to avoid the face where the suggestive cautioning came from.

"If you take him now, you are signing away your right to sue."

The voice was slow and deliberate and very repulsive. This helped to skim off my volcanic emotions in an instant. I spoke downward to those shoes: "We don't do that; we don't sue."

"Well," came the reply, "I just wanted to make sure you understand that once you take him, you will have no case."

My husband stepped in. "That's okay, we don't intend to sue!"

At this our little guy became very much himself. He clung to me with those familiar, welcome hugs and waved his hands around bye-bye to everybody.

A chorus answered back sweetly: "Bye-bye! So you want to leave us? Okay, bye-bye, miracle boy!"

We went through the protocol of dismissal with vibrant joy splashing all around us. As if in a dream, we kept going toward the next step for his release.

"Bye-bye!" Richie kept repeating to everybody we came in contact with in the hospital.

We told our story to whoever would listen. I don't think there was anyone who disbelieved or doubted what God had done. No one cared to argue our explanation. It was heaven on earth! Who would not want to bask in the glory when it comes around?

"I'm so glad for you," said the lady in the business office. "Now, how do you want to pay? By check or…" she asked even though she knew the answer.

The numbers were staggering for a one night stay! But for the first time in my life, it did not faze me to look at such a large bill.

"The God who did this," pointing to my smiling boy, "will also provide for the payment." This statement was fulfilled in a most marvelous way a couple days later. It still amazes me how I spoke those words with such confidence as if it was already arranged. In reality it was, we just did not know how yet.

The lady did her job in presenting payment alternatives, and then she added: "I would strongly recommend that you secure some money in case later he would have complications. This is not greed; it is common sense."

By now we had practice at this. We affirmed that this healing was perfect and complete and to follow her counsel would be acting as if it was not.

At this point our precious boy broke up our vain conversation with his urgent "Bye-bye!" and we got out of there as quickly as possible.

The December air was crisp and invigorating. The glorious sky was bluer than ever. The palm trees were clapping, and the birds were singing to us a triumphant song of great victory, calling to echo our joy into every place.

As we drove over the beautiful Skyway Bridge on our way home, the water sparkled with dazzling cheer under us.

The world was turning again.

Our God Is the Almighty

Together at last, our family was united again!

As if after a torturous hopeless journey, we met again, knowing that what we went through was nothing short of a miracle. We were holding each other, not getting enough of one another, celebrating, shouting, jumping for joy, unwilling to go back to "normal" ever again.

We had to repeat the story to our two older children over and over. All of us were renewed and refreshed in such an unexpected way. We kept talking, laughing, squealing, and thanking God.

How real we were! How true our praise was! How hungrily we wanted to have more details of the past forty-eight hours.

Like a glorious puzzle, we came to recognize a breathtaking picture, eagerly fitting the pieces together for everybody to enjoy. And everybody involved had their awesome point of view and special version...so different, yet every piece fit together perfectly.

Even the struggle I experienced at first—trying to get some rest after the sleep and food deprivation—turned out to be a very important part of the puzzle. To my dismay, when I finally went to bed at home, I realized that I was unable to relax. I could not keep my eyes closed because the scene at that baptistery kept replaying before me. An unbearable jolt hit me the moment I tried to doze off, popping my eyes open with horror. Nothing helped. My husband tried to put our little one with me to bed so I could feel his living body next to mine, but my mind could not let go. Nothing could put me at ease or expel the involuntary fears that were stuck in my mind somehow.

The thought of reliving that moment sent me into panic. Will I have to live with that memory for the rest of my life? A terrifying nightmare was trying to capture my attention.

Lord, help! I cried in a state of utter exhaustion. *I need to sleep!*

The moment I cried out to God I realized that my Lord was right there with me all along.

Gently, he led me to the place of that torturous memory and made his presence very real and strong...stronger than my fear. We walked up those dark stairs together while my mind was putting up every red flag of alarm that it could come up with. Nevertheless, God's presence overcame every thought and dread. No darkness could stay in his light. In this glow I sensed my Lord's encouragement to look at that dreaded scene, all the while reminding me:

"I am with you; do not fear."

I turned my eyes toward the black water with the floating body, but instead of that dreaded jolt of horror I heard his voice:

"Death is swallowed up in victory!"

At this, Richie's smiling face appeared before me, and I fell into deep restful sleep at last.

"Perfect love casts out all fear!"

After sleeping for three days (I am not exaggerating) and eating earthly food again, I felt like a completely different person. There was such a change in us, including our children, that we had to learn a new way of relating our renewed selves to each other.

One could summarize that we had experienced a revival in the most unorthodox fashion…without a preacher or a tent. We had an encounter with the living God that changed us forever.

We were counseled by our church leaders to keep it quiet for a while. They did not want the story in the news; after all, it happened in their facility. The worried faces turned to relieved smiles once we expressed our gratitude for what God had accomplished in us. The idea of suing was ludicrous and an insult, but we understood. (Not even the church is exempt from this societal disease…to fear greed will be stronger than faith.)

Nothing was lost except our place in the ditch of legalism. After everything was put into order in our minds, we understood that even being in the wrong place can be a valuable lesson. At least now we knew where not to go.

Our gain was beyond what words could express. The treasures that we were given by God after this experience are the lasting kind…invisible, yet more real than the earthly kind.

We had some challenges with relatives and friends who needed an explanation to relieve their dismayed minds.

"What kind of God would allow this to happen?" I heard my exasperated mother exclaim over the phone. Understandably, she had a very hard time with this. Two thousand miles away, separated by the ocean, she suffered the aftershock, and no amount of reassurance would satisfy her. She did not want to accept the idea that it was for our good. "You were good before! As a matter of fact, you were turning so good that you scared me sometimes." Her humorous argument was hitting the nail on the head.

"Exactly, Mother! That is the whole point," I responded in agreement. "My goodness was scary, not only to you, but to Rich and the children... and even to me! It was all fake!"

"What do you mean? You are a church-going perfectionist, raising those children to be angels on earth. You even managed to get your husband to go along with you in all you do. What do you mean 'fake'? How can you say God had to change you? Why?"

"Because I had exchanged my love for God for a desire to fit in with the holy crowd," I responded cheerfully.

"So what... isn't that a part of religion?"

My precious mother lived in a convent in her early youth, a rich little girl who had been enrolled in the best of schools for the wealthy. What she learned there did not work out as hoped. Acceptable behavior and social graces were taught in her place of learning, but there was also an unbearable dose of the "straightjacket religion" that she could hardly wait to be set free from. Her resolve to escape and never again be caught in that life of gracious hypocrisy kept her at a cautious distance of any and all forms of religion.

That is why she was so apprehensive about my

so called "transformation." She did not want me to become like those "stiff old maidens," as her teachers were referred to, who were full of that awful strength that condemns with the stare of the "evil eye."

In a way, she saw it happening to me after the initial exuberance that I exhibited after meeting Jesus Christ. She was cautiously happy for me when, in my deepest need just before my first child was born, I told her about having found peace with God. But after joining a church of a legalistic bent, the love of the Savior seemed to be put on the back burner, the joy turned sour, the freedom into bondage, and the affection for Christ was exchanged for bitter hatred for sin that had a death-grip on my world. Because she watched all this evolve over the years, it was not an easy task to assure her that I was free again. There was so much to explain and so much to exemplify in real life to convince her of what truly happened in our ordeal with life and death.

But sometime later, when she came to visit us, her heart was finally won over to the wonderful loving God she saw in our lives, who truly worked all things out for our good.

One night she said with the hopeful voice of a little girl: "You know, I like what I see in your life. This is for real. This is a different religion. This is not like it was. You seem truly happy and at peace. I wish I had what you have."

And so she did. Simply, without trying to deserve anything, without doing "good" things or paying a price, she accepted the free gift of eternal life in Jesus Christ by faith alone and met God in person. Her sparkling eyes after her encounter is the sweetest memory I have with her.

"God is talking to me," she would confide with such unparalleled joy in her voice. "You know, the words that I memorized in that convent are coming back to me. I see now what you mean—the Bible is the Word of God, and I know Christ will never leave me. This is so good! Why didn't I listen to you sooner?"

Sooner or later, the important thing is that when she left this world, she did so with an unshakable confidence that her place in eternity was prepared. Our last conversation was full of joy and an expectation of her Savior who was coming to gather her into his mighty arms of love. How thankful I am to know that she is in that place where there is no more sickness but the newness of everlasting life and the celebration of total freedom in God's Kingdom.

There were others who also demanded an answer from us as to how we interpreted our experience for reasons that seemed hard to understand at first.

We heard statements like: "If that is how God treats his people, what is the use of playing the religion game?" Or "You mean to tell me that God did this to you for your own good? No thanks! I could never love a God like that. What kind of God would allow this kind of suffering?"

These outbursts came from those who thought that this miraculous healing was sheer luck…an unexplainable phenomenon…not the works of the Almighty in whom they did not trust to begin with. These observers of our lives watched us for years to see if what they saw was worth having or not…to see if we would last in this so called godly lifestyle, doubting all along the validity or value of our faith in Christ. And now they finally had a case to prove why religion was useless.

Could our words persuade any of them otherwise? Yes! Some of them. But when words could not get through, our lives spoke loud and clear. Drastically and wonderfully transformed, our joy communicated the answer to the question: "What kind of God would allow this to happen?"

The answer: the kind of God who has the power to work all things together for the good of those who love him and are called according to his purposes!

How wonderful it was to watch most of these "unbelievers" turn around sooner or later to behold the beauty of God's plan for their own lives as they answered the call to freedom. How obvious their relief was to have peace at last in trusting this God they so bitterly fought and avoided! How precious were their words of admission that they were finally satisfied with God's answers to their "unanswerable" questions.

The following weeks leading up to Christmas were upon us, but we could not and would not get into the spirit of commercialism. We were jealously guarding our territory in the "secret place" we found ourselves in. No amount of coaxing made us want to leave the contentment we had just being together. It was the first time we had no tree to decorate, no hustle to get everything just right and wrapped, no stress and insane overspending for a "successful" holiday season.

How wonderful it was to be completely satisfied without the traditional substitution of the true meaning of the Savior's birth. We had something much more real than the glitter of man-made lights and merry-making.

On Christmas Eve we realized as a family what the true spirit of celebration was and is all about. That is when the proof of our transformation was unwrapped in our midst like a most precious gift right from our heavenly Father's hands. The last piece was added to the already incredible beauty of this divine puzzle.

Why did God allow this to happen to us? We were to find the answer in a most heartwarming way.

Our oldest son—then about seven-years-old—said it well as we sat around in our empty living room, filled with joy, just watching our miracle boy running around in circles singing: "Hayeyuyah!" over and over again.

"You know," Robert said in his thoughtful way, "this is the best Christmas I have ever had. Richie is the best gift! I don't even want anything…just to see him alive is the best!"

With soaring hearts at his precious statement, we realized that we were one transformed family.

This was a child who used to measure everything by quantity before this experience. Now he too was enabled to become a discerner of true worth. There was such wisdom in our children. We prized this invisible gift far above the visible but fading substitutes of the "real thing."

Our daughter lavished her affections on her little brother, forgetting herself completely. She patiently endured his "baby-games" without complaint, which was a sign of her transformation. Unselfish love was birthed into her heart, and from then on we were blessed to witness a heavenly gentleness flow from her to Richie and to others as well.

She asked a surprising question for a five-year-old: "Will we celebrate like this again? Could we remember this next Christmas? I don't ever want to forget how God saved Richie!"

So we all agreed to make it our tradition to remember the day when we "passed through the waters" and as a family entered into a new land... a realm of thankfulness and joyfulness in our Lord.

This new sort of joy was so completely different from any kind we had ever known. It was like a surprise, a gift dropped right out of heaven into our bare living room. Just like a present that was unseen and never thought of before... like a package that was opened by the invisible hands of our loving Father, we were treated to an amazing experience on that Christmas morning. It happened so unexpectedly.

One of the children said, "Hey, we don't even have any empty boxes to play with."

Somehow this struck all of us as funny, and we started giggling. Then Richie shouted his "Hayeyuyah!" one too many times, and we started laughing and could not stop.

Waves of laughter kept sweeping over us—all of us, even my otherwise serious husband could not stop the hilarious tears running down his cheeks. As if shaken by a most comforting inward motion, I felt all tension melt away from my body and mind.

Then a most amazing thought occurred to me. What if this is the kind of joy the Bible is talking about for us to have? What if all of heaven is rejoicing with us in our freedom and happiness? What if it turns out that divine joy is actually this wonderful…this light…this funny? What if heaven is not that somber hushed-up place that we sometimes fear in the secret place of our exasperated hearts when we have to admit our displeasure at the prospect of a boring holiness for all eternity?

What if God is actually a God of glorious laughter and vibrant lively joy? What if the hosts of heaven "crack up" laughing when we take ourselves too seriously…when we play the martyr or prepare for our pity parties?

What if God was actually in our living room, not in a religiously reverent way, but in a most real and happy way, just partaking of our celebration with us! And there it was…the greatest gift of all!

God with us!

Simply without any drama, we realized that because God's presence of love was our desire, God was with us. And this gift of joy that God so abundantly lavished on us, was unwrapped to present true eternal riches...a gift that was to stay with us, never to wear out or break from overuse.

The gifts of God are forever living and abiding within those who are willing to receive them.

How true! How worthwhile to seek after these!

Let us desire the greater gifts...the ones only our heavenly Father can give. No one will be disappointed with God's blessed presents of peace, goodwill, kindness, and joy.

True, we did not have anything to show—no trinkets, no toys, no boxes and wrappings. But we received gifts that are still with us to this day.

What are we calling this special day in December? We call it *"The day when God came to live with us."*

This was the day when the revelation was given to us that our God is the Almighty, who has the power over death and who gives life that is truly abundant beyond imagination.

Was it worth it? Of course it was!

All glory, honor, and praise to the Almighty God who was, is, and is to come again, when faith is sight and our hope is fulfilled all over the earth in every heart!

What Matters Most

This chapter could be likened to a crown. Just as a crown makes an ordinary man look like a king, so it is with this story and this last chapter. What you read here is the final piece of completion that makes this book worth reading.

There are amazing stories in every person's life. What we do with them and how we interpret them is what sets them apart for specific purposes.

This story has the potential to reveal God's truth that is unchanging and freely given to all who desire to be partakers of such a transformation, as described in this book, without having to go through such an experience as we did.

"How so?" one may ask. "How can you say that?"

Because of what I have seen in the lives of those who understood and believed that the principle revealed in this story is truly a sacred gift to those who long for the reality of a close relationship with our loving God. This is a divine present to those who are willing to exchange religiosity for a vibrant relationship with the living Savior.

Some have expressed fear that they would have to go through something awful too, if they desire a close personal relationship with Jesus Christ. Nothing could be further from the truth. We are not cookie-cutter believers! Our experiences are gloriously fitted to our complex personalities.

Not everybody has to go through a life and death encounter to wake up to God's call. Some are awakened through reading a story like this. A tender, ready heart can prayerfully glean from this message and make it its own, without having to experience a journey like mine. Anyway, the actual distance that this message has to travel is just a few inches, so to say…from the head to the heart.

You see, it is not the content that changes lives; it is the context that matters.

Who is this story really about? What does the true Author convey to you? If your answer is accurate, so will your conclusion and personal benefit be.

This is God's story! It is about his miraculous love for all. The Almighty is the one who determines the value of his story and the power of its impact on you. If you allow God to speak to you in that context, you will be a partaker of the great and glorious transformation just by reading and praying about what you desire. Only the Lord can reveal to you what you need to get a hold of between the lines.

Instead of focusing on the content of this story and letting your mind file it away without touching your heart, which you have every right to do, allow this to be more than just another tale of luck to you. Let the King of life crown this message with his glory so that what matters most can be yours as you respond to his call.

"What is God's call for my life?" you may be asking, as I did some time ago.

Are you ready for the most simplistic yet impossible answer? Here it is: *love.*

It is interesting to note the reactions we have to this word. We all know that there are many interpretations to this invisible state of being, feeling, acting, and living. There is a real possibility for misinterpretations and substitutes for the true state of love, which is exclusively from God alone.

What we have to realize, first of all, is that we do not have the ability to produce love. Therefore, we do not have it unless it is given to us from God. We cannot manufacture it, neither can we pay for it with sacrifices or manipulate it with our legalistic "goodness" and deserve it in any way.

What we may know is whether we have this love or not. Taking a willing look into the mirror of truth in the light of God's Spirit, some of us will come to honestly admitting our total lack of this divine passion, which is the very beginning of the awakening to love as God does.

Here is a simple test of love.

Think of the person who deeply hurt you or disappointed you. If you are fortunate and do not have such a relationship with another, think of a most unlovely human being and admit your lack of love for such an individual.

Could you make yourself love that person?

If you said *no,* you told the truth and there is hope for you. Nobody can truly love another without God's enablement.

Those who are mature enough to believe that the truth does set free will be excited to do this self-examination. They know that it is worth the "trouble."

This love that transforms our lives in a most miraculous way, that casts out all of our fears, that softens our hard hearts and draws us hungrily for more to the one and only who gives it to those who ask, is what matters most!

Dear reader, do you want this love with all your

heart, mind, soul, and strength? Do you trust God that divine love will be given to you just because you ask? Do you believe that God is that good? Do you know that it is safe to love like that?

This again—like salvation—is given by faith, through Christ, as an answer to a sincere heartfelt prayer. Salvation was the first step toward eternity. What is ahead of you is the quest to find the contentment in God's love even now!

It is a free gift, and this is God's calling to you that you may be filled with unconditional love in overflowing abundance.

"But I thought I received that at salvation..." some may insist.

Right! The potential of this love is granted at salvation, but how many of us actually emanate the absolute love from God for others? How many actually give up their conditional "loves" to make room in their everyday lives for the kind of ardor that supersedes those substitute feelings, desires, and lusts that are flowing from a separate source? Where does your life flow from?

Flow...what is that supposed to mean you may be asking.

I have not understood either, why Jesus said to a woman who was thirsting for water:

"...whosoever drinks of the water that I shall give him [or her] will never thirst. But the water that I shall give him will become in him a fountain of water springing up into everlasting life" (John 4:14, NKJV).

Then one day I realized what she was really after. She was looking for true love, and Jesus revealed to her that in her world she could only access conditional love, which would cause her to thirst over and over again. But the true love that Christ offered was to start a spring of love in the very core of her being, that would enable her to experience and be satisfied with the endless love of God from within.

So, the question is, are you experiencing that surge of God's love flowing from within?

These may be big questions, but my guess is that you have this book in your hand because you are ready to grapple with this assessment of where you are coming from when relating to others.

If this story stirred your heart with a longing to abandon your fears and cautiousness in exchange for God's perfect will in your life, dare to believe that those everlasting arms are forever around you. Trust in the love that connects you with God and then with others. This is your inheritance in Christ. Claim your new birthright from your gracious heavenly Father. It is God's desire to flood you with eternal love to abundantly saturate you forever. All you have to do is ask to experience it and then allow God's love to flow to and through you freely!

Ask for the faith of Jesus to permeate your life...the kind of faith that enabled him to say:

"Thy will be done," then actually follow through and lay his life down in total assurance of resurrection in God's reciprocal love. You can use Christ's example when you need to die to unwanted attitudes. Even if you have to lay down ill feelings or fears, trust in God's promise to give you the new attitudes, joyful feelings, and courage that will stream to you with almighty resurrection power.

Ask for God's love to be your heartbeat so that the atonement is more than a theory. Ask that divine love become the reality of your new life now.

Do you long for this refreshing kind of love? As with salvation, a sincere prayer will do.

It is God's will that you be filled without measure. With divine generosity God is saturating you to overflowing goodwill running over to all without hindrance. That is our destiny on this earth...to love as God loves. Nothing less!

Are you ready?

Let's ask our Heavenly Father right now to give us this true love in the manner of Christ.

Father God Almighty, thank you for your everlasting love for me. Revive me to my first love for you. I relinquish all obstructing attitudes of separation, fears, doubts, and pride, along with my agendas, plans, and inabilities that hinder me to love others. I count my misguided efforts at trying to earn your favors useless and dead in Jesus' sacrificial death. I joyfully surrender to your divine purposes from this day on. Your will be done, your kingdom come just as it is in your presence. I am yours, almighty Father. Refresh me, enable me and guide me by God's Holy Spirit. Fill me with your holy love so that it may overflow to all in my world. Thank you, Lord, for forming the character and purpose of the Lover of my soul, your beloved Son, in my life. Amen - (means: I believe it therefore let it be so)

According to your faith, you have received what you have just asked for. So rejoice forever more!

Meet the Heroes

Before closing this book, I would like you to meet some of the heroes of this story. They have a lot to teach us. You see, we were not the only ones who benefited.

This was a journey we did not plan, a change we did not think was possible, and a transformation that was nothing short of the miraculous that affected other lives also in wonderful ways. After studying the testimonies of the men, women, and children who played a part of that forty-eight-hour ordeal, I came to a most amazing insight. This insight came gradually, yet the answer was and is always there in its fullness. We just had to recognize it. See if you, dear reader, can find the word that describes the marvelous key that opens up the door to the secret place of the Most High.

As you read the following testimonies and revelations about the different personalities and their approaches and "styles" of dealing with the near tragedy, try to guess what made some prayers of no effect and why the ones that were answered were effective.

Do you remember that young man at the baptistery door? The one whose eyes were like saucers at that dreadful sight? Who froze and could not come to my aid?

He told me later how the experience changed his life. First, he apologized profusely for being such a "sissy," but he said when he saw my desperate face, he was sure that I was holding a dead body, and he just knew that he could not handle a situation like that. His reaction is not uncommon; it is even understandable. He was so shaken that he ran away from the scene to avert his attention for fear of fainting. With dismay he realized that he could not bring himself to pray either. He just wanted to get back into the comfort of the "niceness" of his life. He realized how desperately he wanted to get the whole sight out of his mind as soon as possible. And then, he woke up. Yes, he woke up to the even more frightening fact that he was a man without a prayer.

He realized there in his car, trying to stuff his face with fast food to comfort himself, that his addiction to being comfortable at all cost was very much like a form of idolatry. He saw how useless he was to what really mattered…to be there for others in their times of need. He told me that in his mind he fantasized that he was able to do heroic acts of service for God. Thoughts like these kept him in a kind of hopefulness about who he really was.

But through this experience, the truth revealed what he was made of…and this time he did not run. He faced the embarrassing fact that he needed to be changed. However, that was only the start. God did more than that for him. God not only took away his idolatrous need for substitutions for comfort, but that drive was replaced with a heart of compassion for his fellow man. After he learned of the outcome about God's miraculous restoration of our boy, he took a courageous step toward connecting with the Source of all courage. Instead of denial, his response to tough situations is from that other Source within. Now he moves unflinchingly by inspiration that he expects from God to flow freely to him. He also knows that with inspiration comes the enabling too.

~

Then there was another kind of reaction. This one was harder to understand at first. Since then I have witnessed this attitude operate in people under different leadership positions. These somewhat glassy-eyed "accomplishers" are so task-oriented that they miss life buzzing by them without even noticing that what they are after is really not what matters most. This person was in charge of the performance, and the rehearsal had to go on—even if it was over "dead bodies." When he heard what happened, he stopped the music for a moment to explain to everybody what he thought had happened, delivered a mini-eulogy about the brevity of life, and quickly asked God to comfort the family at the loss of their child. Then he turned to the shocked performers—my son and daughter included—and told them to sing the next song on the agenda.

Did he expect smiles, too?

Later, when he found out that we did not lose our child after all, instead of rejoicing with us, he felt embarrassed for having been wrong and hurried on to his next task.

Sometimes we mistakenly call this drive "serving God." But because it is void of the most important element, the leading of the Holy Spirit, this kind of busyness does not leave room for the real work of God. This kind of zeal is a consuming pursuit that is lacking the understanding of what matters most. Thank God, his prayers did not pass the ceiling.

~

Next honorable mention goes to the lady who tried to get me away from that dreadful scene in the hallway. She felt so sorry for me and not knowing what else to do, she wanted to separate me from the source of my despair. What she did not understand (having had no children herself) was that I had to stay at my baby's side. There was nowhere to go to get away from my little boy's desperate need for the next breath. She did the best she could, according to her understanding, but when I would not comply with her wishes to leave, she became a bit unhappy about her "good intentions" not succeeding. She prayed accordingly, but thank God our intentions and suggestions are not what move the Almighty. God works his will in spite of our suggestions or demands about how things should turn out and how people should act. When we pray in a mode of "educating God" about what he should do, we are "barking up the wrong tree."

That is how she put it with sweet embarrassed laughter after we had a chance to talk things over. Our experience transformed this woman's prayer approach, and she was very thankful for this change in her life. Before this experience, she was a frustrated prayer-warrior who couldn't get through to God to get her agendas and solutions "approved" by God. She realized that the solutions and plans of the Most High turned out so much better when she "let go and let God." She was glad that God got through to her instead. How good for her. What a good lesson for all of us!

~

Then, there were those precious children. As my firstborn son told me later, most of them never understood what really happened; they just bowed their heads to follow the leader and said "amen" at the end of his confusing prayer. Can we relate? Do we sometimes just go through the motions during a prayer meeting and then wonder what it was all about?

Those in the nursery did a similar ritual when the word got to them. The nursery workers gathered the children to form a circle and told everybody to hold hands while one of the grown-ups prayed. Some thought it was a new game; some listened as if to a fairy tale. Then when it was time, they bowed their little heads and repeated a singsong prayer to appease the "bigger people" so they could go back to play. Do we sometimes rattle down our petitions as fast as possible, obediently following the rituals of the "bigger saints" so we can "get on" with some small talk with one another? I'm not criticizing anyone. I am just pointing out some lessons I have learned while studying these testimonies that were shared with me. These real-life experiences teach important truths about the diverse approaches to prayer.

Did God hear those prayers?

Wait with your answer until you have read the rest of this chapter.

~

This next example is about that mysterious lady who was in the hallway while we were trying to do what we could before the ambulance arrived. She stands out in a very special way. She was not watching the drama. She had her eyes closed in deep prayer, giving me an example to do likewise. Her presence had a powerful impact on me. She stood a few feet away depicting total trust in God…the kind of trust that was not caught up in the way things look on the outside but was totally absorbed with God's view of the scene. She gave me the encouragement to look to God too, instead of being overwhelmed with the way things appeared at the moment.

And even though I could not pray like her, I did look upward and found that my sure hope was in nothing and nobody but God alone.

I never saw her again. I thank God for her to this day. It is interesting how much she means to me even though we never spoke a word to each other. Yet her example spoke volumes in a most unforgettable way. Surely her prayer accomplished much that day. She was instrumental in teaching me to turn from despair to God. She was a light in that dark moment by just being there while being in the presence of God.

~

And now, we are coming to a group of heroes. There was a group of older ladies who met regularly at our church to pray and intercede. Headed by the godmother of Richie, these women knew how to pray, and they practiced it with passion. This was their day to get together on that fateful morning, minding their business in another part of the building, getting their lists together, when word got to them about what was happening in the hallway.

This wonderful woman told me that they were just done talking about the importance of a clean conscience before God when coming into his presence with our petitions on the behalf of others. Instead of coming out to watch, they "got real with God" as she put it. Soberly and eagerly, they put to practice the good sounding theory about "the effectual and fervent prayer that gets results." They confessed their desperate need for inspirational intercession, and cried out to God to intervene on our behalf. They did not stop when it was their usual time to go home. They stayed until they were done. What does "done" mean? I asked her later.

She said they prayed until they felt relieved and had a great peace settle over them. After they left the church they stayed in that prayerful mode, remembering to keep lifting up their thoughts throughout the day as they went about their duties and continued to intercede into the night and until news came about the miracle in the morning.

Their joy was unspeakable and full of glory. They knew they were part of God's awesome plan. You see, they had no problem believing that God would work it all out for good. As a matter of fact, listen to this amazing part of the puzzle. They had a specific request for me. They prayed in agreement that my spiritual eye would open and so focus on God that I would not fall into despair... and that I would remember that... and (Ready for this?) that I would know "*... all things work together for good to those who love God and are called according to His purpose.*" That is what they were led to pray on my behalf.

They did not waste time educating God about what happened and what he should do about it. They did not ask for a specific outcome, either! They simply asked for God's will to be done. They agreed that with God nothing was impossible. They did not have any problem with a miracle or with death being swallowed up in victory; therefore they left it all in the all-knowing and almighty hands of God.

Were their prayers answered? You better believe it! Did their faith soar with us to new heights? Oh, yes! They were one with us in our great delight and joy of what God had done on that glorious morning.

These older ladies, these seasoned women of God, are examples of effectual warriors who demonstrated to us in real life that strength and fruitfulness do not diminish with age. Quite the contrary! When planted at the river of God—his Word—their usefulness in the invisible realms is increasing with every triumphant experience with the Lord of the living waters.

How I love those ladies! Especially the one who led that group into such a triumph. There will never be a time when I can say that I thanked Christine B. enough for her role and godly influence in my life. No wonder Richie renamed her Mrs. Rainbow.

She is one of those friends you may not see for a while, but when crossing paths again, it is like we were never apart.

Friends are friends forever in the Lord! This is not a cliché.

~

This next one in the lineup is the young nurse from our church who performed CPR on our son. At that time, she had just started her family. But since then she has "grown" to be a mother of seven...at least that was the last count at the writing of this book. She is one of my favorite people. There is a deep appreciation for her in my heart. This experience gave us such love for each other that to this day her name gives me a rush of joy. Our friendship started when she literally threw herself into our lives in that hallway and with selfless abandon gave her all as she tried to breathe life into my little boy's limp body.

Her example is of the one who knows when it is time to give it all without a word and when it is time to talk. She was the one who worked diligently until the ambulance arrived...totally focused on what she was there for...giving puffs of air with perfect timing and accuracy. Then she comforted me with gentle pats on my back, talking softly while we were waiting outside the ambulance for my little one to be stabilized for transport. Without thinking of her agenda for the day, she took me in her car in fearless pursuit of the ambulance, assuring me that it was perfectly all right that her car seat was getting soaked from my wet outfit. Her untiring support was priceless as she sought to meet every need she saw around us. God has gifted her with sensitivity and merciful kindness toward others. But the Lord has also given her other gifts, such as writing songs and poetry of great beauty which she composes and sings to the delight of all who hear them.

On one occasion she sat next to me with her guitar and started to sing one of her songs with such awesome beauty that the whole room hushed to silence. As I listened, I felt transported to another place…a place of flowing crystal clear waters. At that moment, looking at her, it seemed to me that I was beholding an angelic being…one who communicates the fragrance of Christ in every place…in every action. This was one of those unforgettable moments, and I wonder, could it be that God granted me the eyes to see this precious friend of mine as he sees her?

As I mused, looking at her singing the words of Christ so sweetly, a verse came to my mind that talks about "the Spirit who gives life" (John 6:63, NKJV), the living Word, whose image we bear as we answer God's call to a life of spreading his beauty with our words and songs. Yes, that is what we can be in this world.

We can, with our breath, bring blessings through speaking God's Word, singing of His glory, or breathe life into a hopeless situation.

Thank You, God, for Sherry W., my beloved sister.

~

And while we are talking about a "life-giving spirit," this wonderful heroine should be mentioned as well: the lady doctor who showed up at the scene at the most precise moment.

She had no reason to be at the church that morning, but she saw the ambulance as she was driving by and was moved to investigate if she might be of any help.

As she pulled into the parking lot, she was met by the rescue team at the door. After she identified herself as a heart specialist, she was welcomed into the ambulance van. She was the perfect person to come to the aid of our helpless boy needing to be stabilized for transport. Her expertise made all the difference at that crucial moment.

What qualifies her to be a true heroine? The answer is so obvious: she cared!

I believe she was moved by the Spirit of God to be there and play such a miraculous part in our boy's life. How I thank the Lord for doctors who are in their professions for God's glory. Their motivator is God in their compassionate hearts, and their service to mankind is unequaled because of that.

Her comment was: "This is what I am here for…to do what I am trained in and then to pray hard for the rest."

Glory to God!

Later, when we talked all these things over with another doctor (who also works for God), he confirmed how perfect everything was working together…even the fact that I was running with Richie's body in the head-down position. Because of that, his airways were cleared for the nurse's CPR, along with my pushes on his chest, until the lady doctor came to complete the rescue effort. A living picture of Romans 8:28 again. All of us give glory to the one who orchestrated these amazing "coincidences" into a marvelous picture of true team-effort on God's Team.

~

This next "team player" should make you laugh, even though his title is "Reverend." Yes, the man of the church…this hero of encouragement, the pastor.

Imagine a pious yet energetic man in his three-piece suit dancing in our hallway, arms raised, twirling and shouting: "I knew it! I knew it! God did it again! I knew it! Glory! Glory! Didn't I tell you?"

As exhausted as I felt after returning home, I had to come out of my bedroom to see this sight. He did not care if he woke us up or if the whole neighborhood heard him. He was celebrating fully with that contagious silliness that goes almost overboard once it is unleashed.

At church in his pulpit, no one would have guessed such behavior from him. But here he was just letting loose with holy hands in the air (never in church), dancing (so forbidden), shouting (well, maybe about brim-stones), now brimming with joy…and so real!

He renamed Richie "the next Mark Spitz…the greatest Olympic swimmer…ha ha ha ha!"—he was slapping his knees and the walls, with his belly shaking. It was a most hilarious sight, so funny that we burst out into wild laughter too, joining his party, hugging, and praising our God.

How precious that memory is: to see the leader of the flock rejoicing in freedom. What a miracle that was.

~

And last but definitely not least let me tell you about *the* hero.

Who is *the* hero?

My husband, of course.

He has his point of view of this sacred story. But he says he is not a writer, so I have to pen these words if we ever want to hear his input. Of course, my account will be biased, but he gave me permission to write whatever I wanted…he trusts me!

And that is what makes him a hero.

Trust.

That is what sets men apart from the true heroes.

He was a good man in the common sense of the word, but this experience shook him up too, and brought some issues to the surface, that were preventing him from a truly heroic life. He was a normal, "proud-to-be- his-own-boss" kind of guy who would refuse to give up his philosophy, even if it meant constant nagging from yours truly.

My desperate attempts to make a "man of God out of him" were doomed to failure from the beginning. I just did not know it.

So for many years, we had this continuous battle going on. Nothing and nobody could help us…no marriage seminars, no counselors, no pastors…nobody!

I wanted him changed to my image of a godly man. He refused, even though I have tried every trick under the sun. He saw through them all. To my utter frustration, he sometimes would play along with me when the "new thing" I was trying on him was pleasant enough (like the "just-love-him" approach). He would line up with my expectations of what a godly husband and father should be...for a while. But the longest he would last was about a week, which was usually the same length that I would last with my "new agenda."

When I blew it, so did he. So as you can imagine, we were not living "happily," and the thought of "ever after" seemed a curse rather than a blessing. Our life, or should we say "the war," was turning out to be unbearable from time to time—all because, as I put it, he was not willing to play his part in the family.

I wish I could tell you that after that forty-eight-hour ordeal he changed completely and that now he is a saint of a man. But I promised to write the truth.

No, he was not the one who changed...I was!

Then what about him? What makes him a hero then?

Well, what makes him a hero is that he trusted God when it really mattered!

He dared to trust that what God allowed to happen to our family will work out for the good of us all. He even believed that I heard from God...and that took real courage after the years of being preached at by an increasingly bitter "helpmate."

When it came down to the moment of making a choice for the life of trust in God or the deadly fears in his own understanding, he turned his back on his fears and dared to face God's mercy being granted to us. Without deserving any of it, he believed in the miraculous power of God's love extending to us. He could have refused "this whole God thing" because of what I had made it appear to him with my insistent demands to measure up. But instead, he rose up to faith and humbly asked for God's promise to be manifested on our behalf. I believe that is what transformed him into a true hero. The moment he refused his dreadful self-talk that caused the cowardly, inauthentic lifestyle for so long, he was set free to expect great things from God.

That is how he could speak up with such courageous authority in the presence of the doctors in the intensive care when they tried to explain away the miraculous healing as an "unexplainable phenomenon." Not intimidated by their superior position and knowledge, he declared that what they had witnessed was the miracle of God.

That was the beginning of his awakening to his call to be a hero of true faith.

As it is with changes that God initiates, we

were not transformed in an instant. But we have begun, through that ordeal, to realize the blessed life that is from God. Being joyfully surrendered to His will, we were led from glory to glory and from strength to strength ever since.

This experience proved to be a cornerstone, a turning point in our lives, individually and as a family. We gave up on being man-pleasers, on legalism, and on false loves. I gave up trying to change my husband and even my children; as a matter of fact, anybody at all. I adopted a motto: *Once they pass the diaper stage, I stop trying to change them!*

Believe me, it works! It is a much better way to spend my time on this earth. Now instead of wearing myself out by nagging people to death, I pray! Yes, it's that simple. Try it!

However, let me qualify what I mean by pray: pray without doubting! That is where the difference is. That is where the difficulty hides...not in the power of prayer or the willingness of God to answer us, but in our practiced ability to trust God, combined with the unshakable grasp that it is not by our strength but by his Spirit that things work out. God is the only one who changes people with success!

All this took some time to sink in, but when it finally did, the change was glorious...in me!

Let me fill you in on an amazing revelation

that I was blessed with as the Lord patiently led me to a place of total freedom from frustration in my relationship with my husband.

One day he was again his "old self," and this time instead joining him by getting into my "old self," I ran to the Lord (to the secret place of my quiet sanctuary…which is hidden behind my locked bathroom door), and was about to set up a pity-party, when the Lord got through to me with that gentle voice. God led me to a place of observation, where he invited me to take a good look at who I really was in that upset state.

You know how we can fool others and even ourselves—but not the All-knowing One?

It was not a nice moment at all. I tried to wiggle out of that place, but I knew that there would be no going on with my Lord unless I first passed through that process of self-examination. So I did take inventory in the warehouse of my life to find a good reason for my displeasure. And when I did uncover the "secret," God invited me to give some reasons why I should have a godly husband, according to my image. Further, I was to give an explanation why it was all right for me to be upset until my dream came true. And, to my dismay, I could not come up with any great line of reasoning for deserving the ideal man, nor a logical case for my victim act. For all the years of our marriage, I dreaded the idea that maybe I married the wrong man, and I was just getting what I deserved.

At this place of self-examination, I realized that my pursuit of this "dream husband/perfect father for my children" was a setup for living in frustration for ever after. Then the question was dropped on me from somewhere (definitely not from me) that stunned me:

"Based on what, are you thinking that what you desire to have is a matter of deserving?"

What a shocking thought. I could not come up with any good answer in reply. Then, seemingly out of nowhere, I discovered something of great value. As soon as I had nothing to say, I was open to hear something new. In that mental inertia I became conscious of the truth that love joy and peace are not earnable. These states are granted to all by God... even to "disobedient husbands"... and when we, "submitted wives" let it flow (even to those unspiritual brutes), that is when miracles can happen in disharmonious and strained relationships.

What came after that is what I could summarize as being humbled "big time."

When I was done with being undone, all I could do was become silent before my God. All my complaints were laid down, and I rested my case in heartfelt surrender. I could almost smell the ashes of repentance around me. Even the dust seemed better than what I thought of that judgmental attitude I had entertained for years in my utter ignorance.

There came a realization that my choice was to go back to that proudly arrogant existence with its frustrations and disappointments or to rise up from those ashes in thankfulness and acceptance of the great gift that I have in my relationship with my husband.

How utterly different these thoughts were! How freeing and good! I welcomed God's revelations to me with great relief.

The only thing I could not imagine was how to face this man whom I have tried to turn into another for so long. What will he think or do if I am not telling him constantly how to live his life?

Well, as you can imagine, he was shocked. He kept rubbing his eyes to make sure he was not having one of those impossible dreams.

And then something totally amazing happened…after a while he seemed to change, too.

Not because I had anything to do with it, even though the humbling idea occurred to me that because I was not in God's way, now at last he could do his wonderful work in my husband's heart.

A lot of time and energy is freed up when we finally give up on doing God's work.

Now, instead of wearing each other out with endless demands for change, we are allowing the changes to be granted by God as we delight in him.

So how then do we live?

Very strangely...very different from the way things used to be...much better than ever before.

I have never been able to pray for my husband with such goodwill as I can now. With all my heart, I want him to succeed in his life, trusting God's purposes for him. He is free from my expectations and restored to his manhood and his right to make the "necessary" mistakes to learn from and to be strengthened by. I released the past from us and instead I wait on God to will in us his purposes to love one another in the beauty of his holiness. This may sound like a lot of jargon, but these words are like guiding lights on my journey. They illuminate my chosen path to follow the call to love my world.

Trusting in God is an easy thing to say. Living accordingly is the most marvelous and satisfying way of life, even if it seems impossible at first. My husband and I have come a long way. These are the words that this "new man" is committed to live by (without my unsolicited help).

"Trust in the Lord with all your heart, and lean not on your own understanding. In all your ways acknowledge Him, and He shall direct your paths" (Proverbs 3:5–6, NKJV).

Because these are the personalized statements from God's inspired Word, we are witnessing the manifestation of these truths that replace the old hindrance of faulty thought patterns. That is what transformation is all about…not about nagging one another to live up to a self-concocted image.

So if we want to stay in the process of being made into the image of Christ, let us make sure we do not go to the wrong places. And instead of making a long list of the wrong places, let me make a guaranteed true statement:

There is no other place than the living Word of God…his presence and his praises…this is the secret place of the Most High on earth as it is in heaven.

That is where and how true heroes live. They courageously stop trying to be better in their own understanding and strength and instead trust and embrace the best, who is the Lord of life, who alone is the Maker of true heroes, and to whom belong all glory, honor, and praise forever and ever.

Beyond Words

...the fragrance of the rose...
the gentleness of a dove...
the power of the mightiest waterfall...
brilliant light...
love that expels all fears...

This is where we arrived at the end of all words. The limitation is humbly accepted by this author, and all I can do is tell you that I wish I could express the awe the love and the adoration that my living Lord God Almighty deserves. At best my words are as inadequate as trying to paint a glorious sunrise with mud. To try to describe one who is so gloriously wonderful...so "other than" anything that can be expressed in the realms of our speech...who is shrouded in mystery from the eyes of unholy motivation, yet is revealed to babes...this one and only...this gentle Lover of our souls...this meek one who is the possessor of all power...this merciful Judge...this Restorer of eternal life to his creation...this Father...this Giver of joy unspeakable and full of glory...this Water of crystal clear purity...this Provider of all of our needs. This one beyond words and expressions...yet, not beyond reach!

One thought of God's presence bursts a song from my heart. That inner eye has seen glimpses of his glory over the years but is still searching after more of him. The genius of his perfect love is that even though one drink, one taste of him gives total fulfillment, yet it also causes a never-ending desire for more. One can never get enough of his living presence. Here is undefiled religion...true Christianity...the state of being that each one of us has to find personally...the relationship beyond rules and regulations...in the divine law of God's holy love for all.

The door to his presence is his Word of truth and revelation. Not books! Not even one like this, because this is still just *about* him. And what we finally understand is that in and by his Word is where we find him as his Spirit reveals the reality of his presence.

That is why it is so essential to ask for the Holy Spirit's help. Without revelation, the Bible is just a bunch of words, stories, poems, and history—like with any other book where readers can miss the writer's intent if they do not understand the language of the author. As many translations and interpretations there are, the only true Translator and Interpreter of the Word of God is the Holy Spirit of God. Apart from the Spirit's aid, the reader is lost to the realm that opens up before a true seeker.

The key to the door is a desire, a hunger and thirst after God. A heart that does not settle for anything else than the reality of God's abiding presence will find that his Word is the one and only substance that leads on the everlasting way to the life that will never see corruption.

To this one, the living Word, belong all the honor and praise to the glory of God forever and ever!

Epilogue

Many years and many Christmases have passed since. Three more precious lives were added to our family. Now we have three boys and three girls on board, and with our Captain, the Lord Jesus Christ, we are on our way to eternity with God. All in relationship with the living God, still learning and growing in his love and grace day by day.

Not all was smooth sailing, though. That was not promised, to the relief of those among us who like the drama of storms, from time to time, on the sea of life. But the words of assurance: "I will never leave you nor forsake you" (Hebrews 13:5, NKJV) held true and faithful through the highs and the lows.

Our God is with us! In addition to that, we truly feel loved by God…and because he is the Almighty, we are in the best company at all times.

Richie is now a wonderful teenager…full of wonder and surprises. He survived the smothering love that we lavished on him in those months (maybe even years) following the incident described in this book. For quite some time, we could not and would not deny him anything. We were very close to spoiling him with our affections.

Does it work to let a child get everything and get away with everything?

You probably know the answer to that one. We have and are still learning how to live with a living proof of God's miracle of love. Our greatest challenge was and is to live a balanced, disciplined life with this child who was given back to us from the brink of death.

One thing is clear about him. He does not conform to the expectations of religiosity, which is a two-sided blessing.

On the one side, he is "real" in his faith; he is not playing church, not even among his peers.

He spurns the idea that anyone would want to play the fake-it-till-you-make-it legalism game. He actually told me that he does not believe that there are any legalists left in this world…at least not in his world. In his opinion, that kind of mindset is the thing of the past. He says, now there are other issues to consider, like the distracted, overstimulated mindset that is taking people's attention away from God and from one another. In his opinion, because of the computer age, believers are facing the predicament of being "entertained to death." I told him to write a book about it, and he told me that one day he will. Then he added with a wink, "And it shall be a bestseller." So, we shall see.

In the meantime he is playing music that most people would find highly unusual from a young man his age, because of the extraordinary style that he developed. After he made it through a season of fascination with the "progressive aggressive" heavy tunes of our youth culture, he discovered his ability to compose a genre, that he calls "classical ambiance," to the great relief of our eardrums.

This new music is comprised of harmonious sounds without words, so as to let the listener uncover the message for themselves. When he calls me to come and listen to his newest creations on the keyboard, it is with expectant delight that I enter into his world. I close my eyes and actually see his music and find myself soaring in unspeakable wonder, as his message lifts me up to reassurances beyond words. When I beg him to make me a CD, so I can listen to his wonderful music whenever I want to, he just laughs quietly, reminding me that "it is not time yet." He says, I am just a normal mother who projects her children's success ahead of their times. So, now my son is the one teaching me patience and balanced thinking. And I don't mind at all.

He is tender toward God and has an amazing discernment about people.

Once he let me in on what caused the great frustration he was experiencing at a youth event. With tears in his eyes, he said, "They don't really worship God…it is all just a big show. I feel like Jesus; I just want to turn the tables over." These words had such passion, yet without undo pathos…just sincere longing for genuine worship for his God, the Giver and Restorer of his life.

On the other side of his unique personality, he does not accept things easily, not even from his teachers or textbooks. He analyzes everything and comes up with some surprising insights.

With his scientific mind he passionately searches out how things work, and with his deep faith in God's order he is looking for answers that only the Almighty can reveal.

"One day he will invent something for the good of mankind." We hear statements like this repeatedly, and we pray that God's perfect plan will be continually fulfilled in his life. There are some unexplainable things about him, too. When he was still just a toddler, he told us repeatedly what he "remembered" from those days described in this book.

"When the helicopter flew up, I saw God," he would assert with sparkling eyes.

"What did God look like?" we asked.

"God had a big smile, and he wasn't old."

Maybe that is where his aversion comes from when he looks at pictures where God and Christ are represented with old angry faces or an emaciated weakly body. "That is just not how it is!" he would dismiss such paintings with embarrassed disdain.

There are notebooks full of his sayings. Obviously, I was amazed enough to record them from his earliest years. Sometimes when I reread those entries I am reminded of the privilege of being a mother, witnessing the breathtaking changes in the lives of our children. Not one is like the other. They all have a unique story to tell and maybe they will someday.

One of my daughters told me that I should include a few interesting experiences about Richie's earlier years. So I took her advice and added her favorite entries from my old worn notebook.

Ever since Richie started to talk, he was able to bring us to tears of laughter. His remarks about himself and others were incredibly amusing. Another thing he did with cute seriousness is rename plants and animals.

"Here, I picked you some goshpens," he would present me with a pretty bouquet of weeds from a secret spot in the garden.

"Where did you find them?" I would ask.

"Oh, over there under the flowbowers," he would educate me happily, always able to delight us with something new from his treasury of discoveries.

But there are some other things I cannot explain to this day. He had several other incidents when God had to step in to rescue him from harm. It did not matter how closely we watched him. He keeps us fervent in our prayers for his safety.

He also keeps us amazed with his predictions.

Still very young, he gazed at me one day, and after a long thought he said, "You have a baby in your tummy!" And to my surprise, I did! Then he told me when the baby would come, and so it was.

One of the most unexplainable experiences was on the morning of September 11, 2001. He had a dream about airplanes and buildings blowing up and people falling from the sky. What made it even more amazing is that I had a terrible vision, too. I was woken up at four o'clock in the morning by an urge to intercede because of an impending disaster over a city in clouds of smoke. But after jotting it down into my prayer notebook, I forgot all about it until Richie insisted that I listen to his description of that dreadful scene he saw in his dream. I dismissed the whole thing in the hurry of the morning. However on the way to our appointment, we listened to the radio, and to our utter dismay it sounded as if what the reporter was describing lined up with Richie's dream. With breathless shock, I looked at him. As he, too, listened to the eyewitnesses' words of that awful disaster, he said quietly, "You see? I told you."

How fervently we prayed. How heartfelt the sorrow was in those blue eyes. But there was a deep search in our hearts, too. What was the reason that God revealed this to our young man? Not that I have an answer. All I could do was sit there in silence, wondering how these things could be.

Surely there are as many answers to these questions as there are readers. I do not claim to have arrived at the place of omniscience…I rather let God reveal these mysteries to me in their perfect seasons.

And now, here is to you, a kind of "cherry on top" on the lighter side of life that will hopefully encourage your heart for the future. This incident happened at the completion (of the first edition) of this book, and it seemed as a perfect closure…for now...until we may meet again through another book.

The other day I called the children into my bedroom for a time of prayer, and, as usual, it started out with a lot of noise, silliness, and teasing. With little success, I was trying to direct everybody's attention away from the twaddle. However, this time Richie came to my rescue when he shouted a very unusual request above the tumult of his siblings' voices that captured our attention.

"Mother, read Acts 2:17!"

Because there were no open Bibles yet, we just teased him like: "Yeah right...like you know what it says. How would you know? Did you memorize it, Mr. Prophet?"

None of us had a clue what that Scripture was about. None of us are scholars...yet! So not knowing any better, we just gave him a good-natured scoff. But he persisted and spoke with a kind of hilarious authority, mimicking a prophet with his finger in the air:

"Thou shall read Acts 2:17...now!" he thundered with his changing boy-man voice. This cracked us up laughing even more, but my curiosity was awakened to check if there was more to his words than just fun and jesting. As I looked up the Scripture, my glee turned to a flood of unspeakable joy, once again sensing that the living One was speaking to us through his Word, saturating us with sure hope to rise in our hearts for the days ahead on this earth.

Be blessed as you read these words from God concerning the times we are now in:

> And it shall come to pass in the days ahead, says God, That I will pour out of My Spirit on all flesh; Your sons and your daughters shall prophesy, your young men shall see visions, your old men shall dream dreams. And on My menservants and on My maidservants I will pour out My Spirit in those days; And they shall prophesy. I will show wonders in heaven above and signs in the earth beneath... before the coming of the great and awesome day of the Lord. And it shall come to pass that whoever calls on the name of the Lord shall be saved.
>
> Acts 2:17–21 (NKJV)

What followed the reading of these words was a Christian parent's dream come true. I felt privileged to witness all this like an observer on the outside of a circle of young people representing the future. The silliness subsided, and a sweet reverence filled my rambunctious family. Their prayers were big... God sized... full of genuine goodwill for others and a joyful expectation for the days ahead.

How I longed to join their simple yet great faith. Then I thought, why not? After all, that is the kind of faith that lets us enter into the kingdom of our Almighty Father on earth. Thankfully, I remembered that with God we do not get too old to have that precious child-like faith. So I joined them in their vibrant requests for a world that is full of God's love and joy for all.

As for me and my house, we hope and pray for a new generation of young people who truly know the living Savior, who enjoy being in God's presence and because of that they are eager to seek him first in all things. What I learned that day is that if we bother to pray, we might as well pray big…like for a world-wide revival!

How about you, dear reader? Will you join in prayer for our young ones? Let us embrace their simple faith that will not be put to shame but will surely be fulfilled. May it be so for all of us, young and mature…you know, we never grow old in God's miraculous love…(but that is a another book, waiting to be written).

Allow me to invite you to express your insights or decisions that you had while reading this little book. Was it worth your time? How did God bless you through our sacred story? I have provided an email address for your replies.

Please send emails to Invitation2u@juno.com or send mail to First Love Revival Ministries P.O. Box 17354, Sarasota, Fl. 34231

BONUS SECTION

The Promised Afterword

(FOR THOSE WITH MORE QUESTIONS ABOUT HOW TO ENTER INTO A RELATIONSHIP WITH GOD)

First of all, whether you believe it or not, you are already in a vital relationship with God, the Creator of your life. Every day, you were and are given countless and undeniable proofs that there is more to you than a physical apparatus that can breathe and think. What is that "more"?

If the story that you have just finished still left you wondering, this is another attempt to show you (or remind you of) another aspect of your wonderful complexity, which is the part of you that can make contact with the Source of your existence in a personal way. And because some of us need it spelled out in black and white before "signing on the dotted line" to settle an issue of great importance, you will find here a series of insights that could be helpful to you in your quest to enter into this most sought-after relationship with the living God.

Whether this information will benefit you or not is up to you. The decision is yours. If you have read this far in this book, I can safely assume that you are sincere in your seeking. (Of course there is a possibility that somebody is reading this section with other motives, but I am not talking to them.)

I figure you are intelligent and able to make the best choices when you are presented with the timeless facts about eternal life. In other words, this exchange between us can work out very well.

The following section is dedicated to you who desire to know more about a personal connection with the Creator of everything that you perceive with your senses (Genesis 1:1). It is an honor to give you something to contemplate, to provide you with thoughts that you could include in your arsenal of truths. This section may even be helpful to you when you arrive at a place of decision.

Now, instead of gushing forth what I have to say on this subject, may I invite you to pretend with me that we are having a face to face conversation…as if we were sitting together, maybe under the shade of a wonderful tree, or strolling across a bridge.

What you are about to read is like a transcript of an actual conversation with a genuine seeker who appreciated our experience together and who is reaping marvelous benefits from it to this day. It is possible that you will be able to relate to some of the following questions and therefore will deem it a worthwhile investment of your time to read on.

Let us suppose that you are really interested to hear my ideas, and I will pretend that you are asking your big questions. And because we have all the time in the world, we can talk at length, about all the things you want to know about God from the beginning. Let us expect that as a result of our discussion together you will come up with some good answers for yourself.

We may even allow some pauses here and there as you feel the need to contemplate what you are "hearing." The references in the parentheses are "addresses" of the Scriptures that you can check out later. I have provided these so that you may have confirmation of what I am saying. Of course this would only be of value to you if you believed that the Bible is a trustworthy source of truth, in spite of its archaic reputation among those who never read it.

For now I will assume that you believe me when I say that my God is the God who communicates clearly. I believe that there are no limits to God's ability to get through to us. Therefore the question is not so much whether you are listening or not. The real question is: do you have an ear that hears God? Obviously this query is not about the physical sensor of sound in your head; rather it is that inner ear that is able to receive inspiration from another realm.

When God affirms to us that we, human beings, are made in God's image, in God's likeness, (Genesis 1:26)...how does that sound to you? When you hear such a statement, does it thrill you in such a way that you want to hear more, or do you have a dilemma with it?

I will pretend that you were delighted to hear the above assertion and now you want to know what it means to you personally.

So I would tell you this: you, in God's image and likeness means that first and foremost you are a spiritual being who originated and then emerged from the invisible realm of God's Spirit.

How do you know? - *you could ask.*

> If you would read the Genesis account of creation, you would notice that all things were created by the spoken word of God. As God intended —in the invisible realm of the Spirit—to create something wonderful—let us take you for an example—the idea of you

emerged, and an expression was released into the invisible realm of God's mind. This expression or image of you condensed into God's spoken word resonating with almighty power, which launched to accomplish you, the being that God originated in the beginning...and behold, the visible manifestation of you appeared, according to God's desire. You came forth from the invisible into the physical realm.

Is this how the first humans were created also?

Mankind was created in the same order. The intent, the word and the miraculous materializing power of God's will is manifested as a physical form, which contains the eternal being created in God's image.

Was this original human different from us?

At the core, each individual was a spiritual being with mental and physical capacities, harmoniously blended, moving freely in the spiritual, mental and physical realms. This human being was meant to exist in all these realms simultaneously in perfect unity within, and consequently, in perfect agreement with the outer creation as well.

Unity...harmony...that sounds good, but when

was that kind of idyllic pleasantness in a human being?

In the beginning. When God saw the finished product of divine desire, God declared all of creation "very good" (Genesis 1:31).

Your emphasis seems to suggest that there is more to this expression. What does that mean "very good"?

This expression in the original language is "ardently-good," meaning that there was no opposite quality to what God made. Everything God created was passionately perfect and flawless.

Even man?

Man in God's image is perfectly good or "good-good"...perfect and flawless.

Then what happened? Where do the obvious imperfections come from? Did God mess up or did we, humans, mess up?

God is unchangingly perfect, in which state there is no messing up. The holiness of God is understood by inspiration, so do not let it bother you if this statement seems more than your mind can grapple with at the present. The insight will come to you as we progress in our conversation. But let us go back to the other part of your question. According to the Creator's intent, man lived in a perfect environment as a physical representative of God's presence on earth. God's creative genius surrounded man with endless varieties of "good-good" provisions to nourish man's body, mind, and spirit for all eternity. In the middle of God's garden stood the Tree of Life, providing man with the fruit that would maintain man's life forever. In that same vicinity, God allowed another tree to exist, that was off limit to man because of its destructive effect on human life. It was called the Tree of the Knowledge of "good-evil" (Genesis 2:9). The first tree assured human life forever, the other warned of the possibility of separation and death…or as it is expressed in the original language "death-death" (Genesis 2:16–17), a state of perpetual dying.

That's an easy one…right? Who in their right mind would want to choose to eat something that could cause such consequences?

It is easy for us to say from our vantage point, however we have to take into consideration that there was no concept of death in the mind or experience of man yet. The effect of "good-evil," which is "death-death," had not been manifested yet. Man saw only "good-good" in all things.

Sounds like positive thinking. Some people say that is the key to happiness...but to me it seems more like "mental snake-oil"...rather than the "master key" to the good life. I find it ludicrous to try to practice good thoughts in a bad situation.

What man saw in the original order was not induced by positive thinking either. "Good-good" was the reality of man's existence. Man did not have to work or practice good thoughts for the good life. Happiness was a constant and automatic provision in the creative array of man's life.

What a life that must have been! Why would anyone even think about messing it up?

When faced with the choice between "good-good" and "good-evil" there was no contrasting experience to determine the outcome of the wrong choice.

I know I would have chosen life...the "ardently-good" kind of life...

Why?

Just because of God's warning. If I had such a

close personal relationship with the Creator who created everything so good, I am sure that I would trust that God knew best...and I would not want to go against the rules in my "good-good" world.

That is a very honorable sentiment. What we find though in (Genesis 2:18) is that God uttered something unheard of up to this point. God looked at man and said: "Not good..."

I knew something like this was coming. But I thought you said man was "good-good" from the beginning. What went wrong?

Nothing went wrong...yet, there was something about the state of man that was not good. It was not good for man to be alone, or in a state of self-reliant autonomy. Man, in the likeness of the self-existent God, was capable to exist autonomously.

Oh, there was only a guy at this point? No females around?

This may seem a surprising puzzle at first. The human being, mankind, was created male and female originally (Genesis 1:27) in the image of God (or Gods in the original language—Eloheem—this is one of the names of God in the majestic plural, referring to the

God-head that is divine multiplicity in perfect unity).

Now that's a novel idea! Are you saying that humans were male-female in their original state?

The Bible suggests that (in the original language)...and it will make perfect sense as we progress in our conversation. Not only that, but it will be clearing up some misconceptions about our original spiritual character and physical nature and how we may relate to one another more successfully in our human relationships with one another.

All right, so what is the significance of this to me personally?

The significance is that potentially we are, you are, similar to the Godhead, endowed with the capacity of multiplicity in your being. When all the aspects of our being are united and connected with the source of our existence, we are all one, connected perfectly, and all things work together well.

That is good! Isn't it? I would not mind "being one" with the God who is making everything good.

Certainly, that kind of interdependence is very good; moreover it is also the essential base of all harmonious relationships with others.

Well now, being one with others...that is a leap I am not so sure about. That would be a little too close for comfort for me.

Not so in the original order. In the beginning unity and closeness was more natural than separation. You see, this autonomous sovereign human was capable of complete self-sufficiency within, and because of that, mankind had no desire or need for a relationship with the physical realm outside of "his/her" sphere (Genesis 2:19–20).

Kind of like a person who has everything possible in his own house, therefore finds no need to relate to the world outside of his own walls? I can see why that state of alone-ness or independence God would pronounce not good. So what did God do?

What would you do?

I would tell that independent snob to open his/her eyes...and smell the roses on the outside of his/her walls...but I bet God had a better idea.

Well, God caused man to fall asleep, and in

that state of unconsciousness, God separated the human into two parts. After that, God presented the female to the male part (Genesis 2:21–22). Allegorically, an important part was removed from the self-sufficient man's house and taken outside of his domain. This caused him to turn his attention to the outside world where he would find what he was now lacking within.

That must have been a rude awakening!

Not at all. They were thrilled to be able to see each other, to cling to one another, to celebrate their differences, to be unashamedly transparent in their delightful relationship in which they could come together in spiritual, mental, and physical unity. You know the sweet game of seeking and finding each other; the exuberant joy that comes from encountering someone who is so close to you, the pleasures of boundless harmony etc. This was the beginning of human relationship as we know it.

Or as we would like to know it. In my experience most relationships start out pleasant enough but all too often that flavor is lost after a while. What was the point in all this in the beginning?

This was the needed motivation for relationships to unfold in every realm, for the expansion of the race and so on. Now physical man was in search of a mate to find completion and fulfillment (Genesis 2:23–25). Together they would rule over all creation in perfect harmony and godlike authority.

So far so good. It sounds like a pretty awesome plan for a good marriage. They should have lived happily ever after?

"Happily ever after" is the grand plan for all human marriages. But there is more to this amazing union. You can find out about this in more detail later, but for now let me give you a foretaste of a mystery about marriage. It is a symbol of our eternal relationship with God as it is hinted in Ephesians 5:32. But we are not there yet in our conversation. We have something else to talk about first.

Okay. Let's talk about the bad news then. I can feel it coming. So what went wrong with the plan?

Nothing.

But we are not living the "good-good" life. It is quite obvious that something messed up the orig-

inal order. The happily ever after lives are only in fairy tales...or in the fantasies of the naïve.

You are leaving out an important group though. There are people who have been restored to God, who live happily ever after in reality.

In this world? How can anybody be happy amidst so much unhappiness all around? I don't think there are any of those happy people left.

There are plenty of people in every generation who find the way, who know the truth and who live the good life. You can be one of them today.

Well, that would be a miracle! What would I have to do to join the ranks of the "happily restored"?

Instead of joining ranks or doing anything to make it happen, simply believe what God says.

That's it? Wouldn't that be a little too easy?

Yes, that is why it is so hard to believe it. God's answer to our human predicament is so simple that very few are willing to accept it.

Well, maybe it should be made more difficult then...so people could believe it.

That is what most religions are doing...quite successfully. They do their best to present different ways to find the good life, but the problem is that the real message of connection with God and one another gets lost in the barrage of conditions for God's favor.

All right then let us not go there. Let us talk instead about the real problem and the real solution then. I bet they disobeyed God and ended up eating of the wrong tree...right?

Yes, but it happened as a result of a set up that the human pair was unable to avoid.

How so?

A friendly looking creature challenged the woman into making a deadly mistake. The serpent, a representative of the "good-evil" knowledge, deceived her with a "good-evil" question that seemed innocent enough but was laced with a misleading idea. This covert attack was directed at God's character first and foremost, but it also had the element of testing the woman's allegiance to her Maker. When the snake asked the unsuspecting woman if God really said that they should not eat of "any tree" in the garden, what seemed a misinformation, turned out to be a malevolent trap. The woman, being "good-good" did not see the evil in such a suggestion; therefore she tried to clarify what the snake said, by correcting it. She did not do a good job of quoting God's word though. She added something that God never said to them. When she assured the snake that God forbade only the tree in the middle of the garden, she added that even touching the fruit from the "knowledge of good-evil" would cause death. To this the snake presented her with one of the "good-evil" half-truths, convincing the woman that she would not only not "die-die" if she ate of it, but she would actually greatly benefit from going against God. The snake explained that eating the forbidden fruit was the key to godlikeness and wisdom, which again was a truth coupled with a lie, which always spells disaster, even to this day.

I never realized that a question can contain a misleading lie. Now I can see how an offer for greatness can lead to a fall. Did the woman forget who she was? She was supposed to tell the snake what to do…not vice-versa…she was supposed to rule over the snake, not take counsel from it! The offer did not even make sense! They were already like God! Were they not?

The man and his woman together—in unity—were already in the likeness of God, therefore they did not need to know "good-evil" to become what they already were. The real bait was the idea that she could be like God by herself, and he could be like God by himself...without needing God or each other, thus the idea of separation was introduced as a viable option for mankind.

Sounds like one of those secrets of our time...the "new" discovery that promises everything under the sun as long as we believe that we are gods who created the universe.

Well, again, it sounds good to some because it is a half-truth. Partially it is truth, because we were created in the image of the Creator, but no sane person would actually believe that he or she spoke the Universe into existence. However we do have creative power to create our own realities.

You think so?

With our intents, thoughts, and spoken words we do create our individual experiences.

How?

For an example if my intention is to love somebody, my thoughts will focus around pleasant ideas, and my emotions and words will be lovely accordingly. What I speak then causes the good feelings to expand and to rise in an overflow to others as well, which in turn affects my surroundings also, thus I am able to create a pleasurable reality.

But what about the unpleasantness in life...who creates those realities?

The same is true with opposite intentions...and their effect on our surroundings. Most unpleasantness is created "by default" by those who allow unpleasant thoughts to dictate their words and actions. Practicing positive thoughts and saying positive words does have a much better effect on our environment than the negatives. However, what really matters is what the intent of a thought is, where a thought originates from. If somebody is working really hard to think only positive thoughts, but stays separated from God, no amount of positivism can compensate for the lack of relationship with God. Even though the techniques of positive thinking appear to be working, there is a persistent lack in them. Trying to find fulfillment apart from God is like trying to quench a big thirst without water. Substitutes may work for a while but nothing can take the place of the real thing.

I can see that we would be buying into fads like that...but they? The first couple had it all...they did not need to be more like God...they already were!

Neither did they need the kind of wisdom that the snake promised would enrich their minds. The expectation to become more intelligent, through the knowledge of positive-negative thinking pattern, was a set up for a huge disappointment to the woman.

Where was the man? Was he napping in the shade? That would be typical. Why was he not paying attention?

The man was with his woman, listening to her telling him about what she heard from the snake. That could have been the man's chance to turn to God and make a choice based on what he heard about this issue from the beginning, but he was not able to see through the deception either.

Did they forget what God said? I am beginning to wonder if they actually loved God.

That is why this had to happen, according to the bigger plan, as part of their development into the true representatives of God's character and purpose on earth. What God intended for them was happening either way, which was to develop loyalty, love, and voluntary God-dependence.

But I thought they had that already in them at creation. Were they not perfect in every way?

In spite of their created perfection, the woman and her man fell for the offer to imbibe the knowledge of separation.

Why?

Because love, loyalty and voluntary dependence on God cannot be created; it unfolds through experiences and choices. That is what freedom of choice is all about. Not between "good" or "evil," it is not even between "good-good" or "good-evil." The ultimate choice is atonement or separation. And only those who have experienced separation can wholeheartedly choose restoration. And those who experience the restoration rise up to loyalty and are connected in true love and appreciation. God-dependence then becomes the treasured state of being.

Well, then obviously she had no idea about any of this yet. So she just ate it all up…worm, hook, and sinker…right?

And when she did, she drew into her being the knowledge that she did not expect.

I wonder if she had a premonition or at least a creepy feeling as a warning.

The moment the woman considered the "good-evil" knowledge she was already in potential trouble, she just did not know it. Being still "good-good," she could not see anything wrong with the forbidden fruit. It looked good to her. The trap was set and she walked right into it, with her man along, who was also totally oblivious to the fact that this would be their last picnic in the glorious garden.

After they ate the forbidden fruit, their eyes still beheld the same scenery, but they could no longer see the perfection and the beauty. Their bodies were still the same magnificent vessels, but now they felt an urge to cover up in embarrassment and shame. They could hear the lovely voice of God calling for them, but they hid from God's presence in terror. They started the blame game and the accusations and would refuse to take responsibility for their actions. Enmity and fear ruled in their hearts, life became full of pain and endless toil. Their once joyous relationship turned into a desperate power-struggle. Instead of speaking blessings they spoke and heard curses. And to top it all, they had to accept their mortality as the inevitable conclusion of their futile existence apart from God (Genesis 3).

What a bummer…it sure sounds familiar. It is a close description of the human race. All this misery because of that disobedience…

The real problem was, and still is, unbelief induced by wrong information. The act of disobedience is just an outward show of what is lacking in the inner man. This is how it goes to this day; the moment we exchange the knowledge of God for another kind of knowledge, call it wisdom or intelligence, if it causes unbelief in God, we are prone to operate in a state of alienation from God. This is what sin means: a state of lacking God and the corresponding godless acts that follow. That is why mandating or forcing change in outward behavior, without inner reconnection with God, cannot succeed. Only by inspiration from God can we make "good-good" choices within. Only inspired actions can successfully replace wrong actions.

Did man's choice mess up God's order too? What about the original plan? Is it ruined?

Nothing is messed up or ruined that God cannot restore. Even unbelief and wrong choices are in order to facilitate good choices and unshakable faith. God was not surprised by the fall of man. It was part of the big picture. All of this is working out perfectly. Mankind fell for a wrong relationship, but will never again do so after being restored.

So God is not angry with mankind?

Would you be angry with a child who touched the stove after your warning? Or would you rather have mercy and compassion and do your utmost to comfort and help the healing process? The idea of an angry god is conjured up in the minds of angry man. That is a god made in man's image.

That explains all the contradicting images presented by the religions of our world. How can they all claim that their image is the only right one?

Because God is perceived according to the prevalent information that man accepts as truth. Just because everybody believes in a god of anger it does not mean that they are right, yet many of us accept a "truth" just because "everybody else is doing it." This is why it is of utmost importance to find out the knowledge of God from God, not from man.

Yeah but what if I don't have any idea how to "hear from God"? Maybe my ear, that could hear God, is disconnected. Obviously someone will have to tell me the secret, so I can know what it takes to hear from God.

You hear from God by faith, which brings us back to the beginning of our discussion. All you have to do to reconnect with God is to believe God's truth for yourself.

How can I have faith in God if I cannot hear God's truth for myself?

Faith in God comes by hearing God...that is true, but here is the good news for those who cannot yet hear from the spiritual realm. Hearing comes through the living Word of God (Romans 10:17). As you hear what I am reading from this Bible, which is the written form of the message, you can perceive what God is disclosing to you from beyond the ideas that you have conjured about God. When you turn in God's direction and listen attentively to these words, you will recognize the communication that will in turn revive your inner hearing.

I know that we are not talking about my ears and we are not talking about my conglomeration of thoughts about God. But then what are we talking about? What else is here?

It is not what…it is who. The question is who else is here?

Now it sounds like we are talking about a person. Are you saying that we are having invisible company here?

We are in God's company at all times. You and I are having this conversation in God's presence. God is with us…right here.

You seem so sure of what you have just said. Why can't I?

This is not hard to follow, but some of us have a harder time with the idea of a spiritual entity being present from beyond the realm of the mind. And the reason it is so hard to accept this is because…

…we lost the connection…so God really told the truth about getting lost…I see now. So the knowledge of "good-evil" did cause spiritual disconnection. Could that knowledge be replaced by the knowledge of "good-good," so we can go back and be restored to our spiritual origin?

Well, there is something even better. We do not go back to what was. We are going forward to the kind of relationship with God, with ourselves and others, that is safe from falling for the knowledge of "good-evil." After we awaken from the nightmare of separation we will no longer be entrapped by it, no matter what temptations are offered.

Why not just cut down that allegorical tree and eliminate the source of temptation altogether?

God created all things, including the forbidden knowledge. The solution is not eliminating the tree that offers the wrong choice. The real solution is to develop a power within that is superior to the deceptive desires that would lead to separation.

Oh, so the problem is not with what God created? The problem is with our desires. I have often wondered what it is about us, humans, that we are captivated by the things that are off limit; like the proverbial cookie-jar that suddenly has almighty power over a child?

Without our fascination with and desire for that which is forbidden, the knowledge of good-evil has no power whatsoever. It is our destiny as human beings to develop a greater power than that of temptation.

That is a mindboggling potential; being above temptation. So we have to become stronger than desire?

Actually, it is not about being stronger than desire. There is nothing wrong with strong desires. This is about discovering your ability to choose life when presented with other alternatives; to desire to be in unity rather than to be separated. This is about the redemption of your power to choose.

But I thought I always had that. As a human being I always thought that I had the right to choose.

The right yes…but how about the power to choose and then live based on that?

Oh, I see what you mean. There is a huge difference between having the right and having the power to live based on my best choices. I must admit, there is a huge lack in that department. I wish I had more power to live according to my better choices.

You wish? Well, listen to this: Your wish is God's command!

What do you mean? That sounds like God is some sort of genie…

Exactly! I am glad you caught that. It sounds wrong because it is backwards. Nevertheless, what I was stating is a wonderful fact that will thrill you once you see the words in order. So, here it is put the right way - God's command is your wish–how about that?

What is that supposed to mean?

It means that there is a deliberate agreement between God and you.

Well, that sounds great, but to tell you the truth, my wish is more on the selfish side. I want power to live right because I know it would feel so much better to me personally...not necessarily because God commanded it. I never realized that an agreement with God could be what I really wanted.

Can you feel the difference between what your life was in the state of separation from God, and what your potential is now, in agreement with God? (pause to think)

Yes, I feel thrilled...I just became aware of a kind of excitement at this thought.

That is how the call of God is. It is a distinct joyous sensation that emanates from within, that also draws your attention to God's realm simultaneously. This is how it feels to hear from God.

I hear you. Some of the things you say thrill me, but how much of what you are saying is coming from God?

That too, largely depends on you. Let us say, I may tell you something nice like, God loves you. As you hear me with your physical ear, you let it into your mental realm to be processed. Either you accept it and smile at me or choose to doubt it, roll your eyes, and then forget all about my words. But if you wanted to find out if God really loved you, you would have to take my words and allow them to enter the realm of faith. As you waited there expectantly listening to God's response, you could "hear" those words confirmed to you from God. Then it would no longer be my words to you, but rather it would be the word of God, through me, to you, from God. Once you "get" those words from God, you would know my statement to be true without a shadow of a doubt…even if someone said something else that was contrary to that truth.

So spiritual hearing is really up to me? I thought that it was just a cliché…to shift the responsibility on me, in case what you are saying would not

work for me. Now I understand that having an ear to hear is a kind of willingness to bring what I am hearing to God for confirmation.

Yes, and that is also the place where heaven and earth meet; the realm where the connection is made with God's Word, who has been waiting for an audience with you.

God's Word?

Yes, God's Word, who is, in spiritual reality, a divine Person.

Well, then let us turn our attention to this Person. I am ready to hear the Word of God.

Actually, you are the one responding to God's invitation, at last. This is the turning point of our conversation and your life. What follows this meeting is your rebirth or awakening from spiritual death. You will recognize God's presence as you hear the Living Word.

Who is the Living Word?

You may have heard about him, which can be good or bad for you, depending on the description. If it was from someone who claims to know him, the description could be helpful, but if it was false, it could be frustrating. Just like you can be sincere when describing someone but at the same time you could be sincerely wrong, the same way, many describe this person based on their opinions, which could be accurate or totally off. Add to it, your preconceived ideas, and you could lose interest in meeting him before you had a fair chance to make a choice based on who he really is.

I can see that. That is a good point. I also understand that meeting the Living Word personally is how I can make a real choice whether to believe him or not. So, who is this Person?

Christ, who in Jesus was the physical manifestation of God on earth and who is now, to you, the spiritual connection with the realm of God. This is the one who will tell you about God with perfect clarity and power. Once you listen to Christ with willingness to believe him, you will notice that your inner hearing will steadily improve and your faith will steadily grow also.

That is an awesome thought. So Christ is here now, present in the spiritual realm, and all I have to do is believe that what he says is true, and I will be connected to the realm of God?

Yes. At last you are ready to turn, to listen and to believe.

How long has Christ been waiting for me to turn to God and believe in what he says?

In eternity there is no "long waiting." In God's realm it is now and now and now...and so on. But if you want your mind boggled, the answer is: God has been waiting for this moment before the beginning of time. God has loved you with an everlasting love (Jeremiah 31:3) and sent Christ into this time-space reality, to you, with the Word to offer you everlasting life in atonement. (John 12:44–50)

So Christ, the Word of God was around before everything was created?

Yes. "In the beginning was the Word, and the Word was with God, and the Word was God" (John 1:1, NKJV).

God and the Word are one. Further, listen to this: "He was in the beginning with God. All things were made through Him, and without Him nothing was made that was made" (John 1:2–3 NKJV). This means that you were created by God's Word also, in God's image and likeness. How does that sound?

It sounds similar to the beginning of our conversation when you told me about the Genesis story.

Yes, the two accounts were written thousands of years apart, nevertheless, they are describing the same Godhead. Whether chiseled on stone tablets, at the dawn of human civilization, or penned on papyrus, in another time of history, the written Word of God made it to our time to lead you into all truth now. Therefore, let us ask the Spirit of God to help you hear what God would want you to hear. When you hear God's Word and take Christ into your being, the living Word will start a revival…in you.

That seems a bit farfetched. How could I be elevated to such status…Christ in me?

Not elevated, rather restored to your original purpose. God desires atonement with you.

Why do I have such a hard time believing this? I want to, but honestly I do not feel worthy of such an honor.

Because you are still partially influenced by the wrong information about who you are, like the first generation of the first man. They managed to forget who they were (because of the separating "good-evil knowledge) to a point, where they believed in a false concept of an angry God, who was out to get them and annihilate them at the drop of a hat. They invented endless laws and rules to make the way to God impossible to follow. They believed in other gods, that they made up in their fractured understanding, while still claiming that they were the people of the one true God. With their endless and senseless regulations they prevented sincere seekers from coming to God. Guilt laden, helplessly lost humanity had no way of finding the truth about their eternal purpose. Because they no longer believed in their authentic God, they bought into their fabricated gods with grave consequences. The original joy of life was completely lost to all. Human existence succumbed to the darkness that surrounded them without the knowledge of God.

Not much has changed. People have just gotten used to the darkness a little more. Now we have substitute joys that serve us like artificial lights to lighten our darkness.

That is why God sent the Word, "eternal life," in a human form to us, to give us a glimmer of the light of the life we were created for. This divine, physical human, who as you can see now, was none other than the invisible God in visible form, came to usher in a new beginning for mankind. Not mandating change but rather offering the restoration of the original intent and plan of God. This offer is extended to you too.

Let me get this straight. Christ is God and Jesus is God in the physical form. So in a way the invisible God showed up in a body to be seen by those who could not see or hear God anymore because of being blind and deaf to the realm of God's spirit?

The generation of the original man is in a dead-sleep to their spiritual senses. As we said earlier, God was not kidding about mankind being lost to the reality of their purpose. All we have left operating are our physical senses and our mental capacities, which are malfunctioning because of the separated, polarizing knowledge of "good-evil" to this day.

How is humanity able to function without the spiritual aspect?

Because of lacking the spiritual aspect of a complete being, a substitution was invented in the mind of man. A mind can divide itself and call one part of it god and then pretend to be hearing from God. It is the desperate attempt to have at least a make-believe relationship with a higher power, but in reality it is a vain effort that can only produce a counterfeit wholeness.

The futility of inventing false gods should be obvious, but most of the time those who make them, cling to them because they don't know how to find the one who exists beyond man's thoughts.

Well, I can relate to that. Sometimes I talk to myself as if a part of me was smarter than the other. I ask the other part to tell me what to do, but sometimes that part is dead wrong. I can see what a mess it would be if I made up that the part that seems to know better at times, was God talking to me. But the idea of actually hearing from the God who is always right is very appealing all of a sudden. Can we talk about that?

We are talking about the need for an awakening; spiritual resurrection, mental restoration, and physical revitalization for the human race.

That is a big job! I can see that only God could do all that. So was the person we call Jesus serving as a kind of a carrier or conduit of God's word of life; to give back the spiritual life that they, or rather that we humans, or even closer, that I have lost?

"In Him was life, and the life was the light of man" (John 1:4, NKJV). No human mind could make a statement like this. And if you notice, this doesn't even make sense to the fallen mind.

I am beginning to see! I think I can sense this light of understanding coming to me! This is very exciting! My past dilemmas about life are like a huge dark contrast in the presence of this light. What will happen with my old contrary attitudes toward Christ? Now I am really sorry about wanting to reject this light for so long because of what I used to call "the religion game."

Do not worry about your past. In the light of Christ you will see why you did what you did. God is not easily offended.

But I have some stubborn habits of negative thinking...and many dark fears are lurking in my mind. This is a darkness that has been around all my life...

"...and the light shines in the darkness, and the darkness can not overcome it." (John 1:5, NKJV)...and will not overcome it in your life either. Once the blinders are removed, God's light, in the person of Christ, floods your being and what was your spiritual death and mental darkness, instantly disappears.

It sounds grand. But are we still not just talk-

ing about Christ? What you are reading from the Bible sounds like the account of somebody who is describing Christ. Whose words are these I am hearing? When will I hear Christ himself? Where is he now?

Christ is here, however before you can hear him, these words serve as a preparation for his imminent appearing. Right now we are listening to the voice of one who knew him in person. This narrator was sent by God too with the specific job, similar to the work of a forerunner of a king, to prepare the way in the hearts of those who are ready for his arrival. This voice was describing to you who the Word is.

Yeah, it is like a voice from a different atmosphere... I can feel my attention drawn to another realm as I hear these words. Is this narrator speaking God's word too?

It can be described like a voice that is calling you into a place of focus. It has been described as "the voice in the desert," and it is a good description because one has to be in a place of least distractions when preparing to hear the living Word.

So what I am hearing can be from the written word as well as from the spoken word?

The written word of God is narrated, quoted, and described by many inspired writers, who were invited to make contact with the spiritual realm, who then were enabled to "transpose" what they received from God into words that could be heard and read by others later.

I used to think that the Bible was an archaic irrelevant collection of nonsense.

Because it was…to you, as it is to many who try to read it alone, without the help of the Spirit of God. In your disconnected state, nobody in their right mind could expect you to value its riches and life-transforming potential. Without knowing the spiritual source of those words, they can be of no use to anyone. Except maybe to carry it around on certain days to look respectable or to place it on the coffee table because it fits the décor.

So, there is more to understanding the Bible than just reading it.

We can safely say, without inspiration there is no revelation. Understanding for the Word of God comes from God, to ready hearts.

Does that mean that I am getting inspired and prepared as I am listening to you?

Inspiration is a spiritual movement, flowing from the spiritual realm into the mental realm, where it creates new thoughts and joyful expectations, which then produce joyous feelings in your body too. Inspiration affects your complete being, and it is very good for you.

I feel spurts of joy as we are conversing, but they come and go? I would love to feel more of the joy and less of the old feelings of doubts about what I am hearing.

The good news is that this too is up to you. The more you want of this joy, the more you get of it. All you have to do is remain in a state of readiness to hear from God. Why the joy comes and goes is because, for the most part, you are used to listening to other voices, rather than to God's. On top of it, as you have mentioned earlier, your old mindset that is in a state of double-mindedness has conversations with itself according to the worldview of "good-evil" knowledge. Because the fractured mind cannot hear past its harangue of doubts and fears, it is stuck in the need to control everything and everybody. And a doubting and controlling mind is not a happy mind.

You tell me? I have lived under the tyranny of

double-mindedness for way too long. There is no joy possible there, except maybe the sick pleasure of being right about some ominous predictions. But as of now, I am no longer without a choice. I choose joy! And because I understand that the continuity of my joy depends on who I am listening to, let us stop talking about the old attitudes and turn back to God to hear some more about the Word.

Good choice! Good for you...and for the world around you. Now that you know that true preparation is more than mental consent, you can hear what this eyewitness is telling us about the King of kings, who is about to come to you for a personal visitation.

I can hardly wait! What is the name of this "forerunner"?

The following narrative was written by John, one of the inspired ones. Right now we are hearing from John, about John. He is describing himself in the third person. He was an eyewitness to the long awaited physical manifestation of Christ, or as they called him, Messiah, in the original language. So here is his report.

"There was a man sent from God, whose name *was* John. This man came for a witness, to bear witness of the Light that all through him might believe. He was not the Light, but *was sent* to bear witness of that Light. That was the true Light which gives light to every man coming into the world. He was in the world, and the world was made through Him, and the world did not know Him" (John 1: 6–10, NKJV).

Wait a minute! So there were some who did not recognize Christ when he showed up on earth?

That was not the worst reaction. "He came to His own, and His own did not receive Him" (John 1:11, NKJV).

One day you may want to read the whole story. Right now I am just letting you know how far those who did not receive him went with their rejection of their Messiah. We will continue where we left off shortly, but I think you should know about what God went through among those he created and came to rescue.

In a nutshell, after Christ ministered miracles, healed and taught the people for years, Jesus was rejected by the religious leaders, betrayed by one of his close "friends," and handed over to the occupying forces of the land to be killed as a traitor to his people.

What? That is the most outrageous garbage I

have ever heard! How could they do that? Why did God not wipe them off the face of the earth before they could lay their filthy hands on him?

God could have, but God had a better plan. Remember, first of all, God in Christ exists in perfect love toward all. God, through Jesus, was reconciling humanity to that love and unity. God's desire is atonement, which is impossible for a human to desire without a clear understanding of who God is and what God can do. Jesus, the physical form of the invisible God, was there to communicate with humanity about the grand rescue from "death-death," which was their biggest dread.

Yeah, I remember from the garden scene. God warned them about that, but they did not know what death meant back then.

And most people still don't know the facts about death to this day. Unless a person is connected to God, the fear of death is a constant nagging torment in the back of the mind. But it should not be. There is nothing to fear about leaving the physical realm to be reunited with our source of eternal life. People who are walking with God on earth go through the experience with a smile.

That is hard to imagine. Death has a stigma attached to it as if it is a punishment of some sort.

Yet it is not that, except in the mind that feeds on the knowledge of "good-evil." To those who are atoned to God, the whole experience is kind of a homecoming celebration. However, to those who are in a state of disconnection, the dread of death is doubled…as if it wasn't enough to die once.

Oh, I see. That is the "death-death" idea? How does that apply to us?

The natural death that physical beings experience is what the people in Jesus' day referred to as the "first death," and that was bad enough. But there was something that they feared more than anything. Their greatest terror was and still is the "second death" which gave fuel to more torments than anything else in human history. Some humans are so messed up in their minds that they cannot even name their fear. So instead of calling it what it is, they call this harmful emotion "the fear of the unknown," which is a set up to dread change. These fears keep people in bondage, forcing them to do the so called "good works" to help them escape the horrors of the second death (that is supposed to go on forever and ever). These torments caused another form of cruel slavery to wrong thinking. God sent Christ to set the record straight by demonstrating something that would break the yoke of this ruinous fear in the hearts and minds of people.

But they killed him! Why did Jesus have to die like that?

The seemingly terrible injustice of killing God's Son turned out to be the very demonstration of God's love and willingness to cancel out the fear of punishment and death altogether. God not only showed the people that physical death is not the end of the individual in the eternal plan, but God also made it clear that there would be no second death either, so those who believed God's Word rather than their fears could be freed instantly from the paralyzing effect of tormenting thoughts about what might happen in eternity.

How on earth did God do that? So far none of this makes sense. What good can come out of killing the long awaited "Answer"?

God not only showed up in a human form and spoke their language. God also matched the message to their culture and traditions to facilitate complete understanding of what they needed to comprehend what he was saying. Killing to appease God was nothing new to that generation. Actually, their tradition mandated that they kill animals as substitutions for the death that they deserved every time they broke a law. They believed that without shedding somebody's blood, there could be no forgiveness of their sins. So instead of killing each other off, they substituted their animals in their place. This is the culture and the mindset that Jesus came into, to finally end the empty rituals that could never restore anyone to God anyway. God was not interested in their sacrifices as substitutions for a real relationship. God came to man and demonstrated the horrible error of being satisfied with their sacrificial system. By allowing them to kill him in person, God accomplished an awakening in the hearts of those who saw him die a cruel death on their behalf. At first, those who believed in Christ where devastated by what happened.

I can't even imagine how the people who knew who he was must have felt. It is sickening just hearing about all this. So what happened after that?

Something that nobody expected happened.

On the third day after his death, God simply reentered the physical realm and resurrected the body of Jesus, thus demonstrating another aspect of who he was. They witnessed at last that Jesus, Christ, and God were in perfect unity and this Godhead had almighty power over fear and death. In addition to that, Jesus told those who listened, that in his death he took all their sins (past, present, and future) away and died with them forever. Then he told them the really good news. Without sacrificing another animal, without trying to work hard to deserve it, God was offering all mankind the reconnection of their lives with their spiritual heritage. Jesus Christ opened their eyes to God's heart of mercy and love. Those with restored eyes saw that the door was never locked from God's side.

How about the religious leaders? Did they finally believe who he was or chose unbelief?

Their unbelief was and is to this day like a veil that prevents man from entering into God's presence. But those who believed the resurrected Christ witnessed that veil split apart by the power of divine love.

For the people of God, the old system of fear is obsolete. All things have become new from God for those who believe in the All-sufficient One.

So how do the people of God live in this Godless world system?

By faith alone…which is the most satisfying and fulfilling existence there is.

And how do they function…how do they know what to do in this world?

By simply listening and believing that God not only loved them, but is offering himself to come and live with each believer, just for the asking. God made it very clear that everything was and is and always will be well with those who are connected to Christ.

Wow! That is good news! Did they finally get it?

Not everybody listened and not many could believe that there was such a good God…

So some would still not take God's amazing offer, even in the face of such a miracle?

Some did not…"But as many as received Him, to them He gave the right to become children of God, to those who believe in His name: who were born, not of blood, nor of the flesh, nor of the will of man, but of God."

Children of God! What an amazing simile. That makes me think of God as a father...a good one, a very good one...a "good-good" Father. I want to believe in such a wonderful God.

And if we stay with this analogy, then I can see how Christ would be called the Son of God. Wow! This way of putting it, brings God much closer to the human race...and to me. Now I see why God planned to come in a human form. The physical or flesh-man, that had no will or ability to hear from God, could not receive God's word without a visible physical human form who actually spoke their language. But let us go back to what John had to say in the beginning of all this. So God's plan was for us too...I mean...for me.

That is correct. So, what do you suppose God did for you?

God sent the Living Word?

Yes. "...and the Word became flesh and dwelt among us, and we beheld His glory, the glory as of the only begotten of the Father, full of grace and truth" (John 1:13, NKJV).

What an amazing moment that must have been for John! As I am listening, these words give me a feeling like John really loved God. I wonder what

he did when he laid eyes on the Living Word in the visible form of a human."

"John bore witness of Him and cried out, saying, 'This was He of whom I said, "He who comes after me is preferred before me, for He was before me."'"

It sounds like John was really excited. He must have been full of joy.

Yes. "And of His fullness we have all received, and grace for grace. For the law was given through Moses, but grace and truth came through Jesus Christ." (John 14–16, NKJV).

I bet there was celebration! God on earth! Finally God could let everybody know the good news that they did not have to live in the miserable darkness any longer. Wow! Finally they could see. Right?

Those who could hear what John was saying, yes, they could see Jesus for who he was, and they celebrated. But there were many who refused to believe John, who would see in Jesus only a dangerous character, who claimed what they thought was impossible. You see, they could not believe that God would actually show up on earth in a physical form. They could not imagine that God would stoop so low as to inhabit a human body that they considered base and cursed, rather than the wonderful physical creation of God. The god they conjured up in their indoctrinated minds was an angry taskmaster, who forced humanity to conform to laws and regulations for favors in return. In addition to that, Jesus was a threat to their position and authority, not to mention to their thriving business as religious leaders of the masses.

Not much difference today with the religious folk. No matter where you look, they all have their set of rules that promise the only sure way to God. It amazes me that so many people buy into the religion business: buying favors from God. What a farce! Rules about everything...is that what John was talking about when he mentioned the law that was given through Moses?

The Law that was given through Moses is good and perfect. It was given by God. The Ten Commandments, as those laws are referred to, are a mercy-gift to humanity. Actually in the original language it is called the "Ten Words." These "Words" give specific details about how to avoid the traps of the "good-evil" mindset. In the original language they are simple and to the point. Like a loving note from a devoted father, the Ten Commandments give a list of do's and don'ts about how to stay out of trouble.

Can I hear the list?

Certainly. However it will only benefit you if you hear it as if it were from a loving father. If you hear it with a mindset of "here is the list that you must keep or else," than it will only cause harm. Actually, the Ten Commandments are deadly to someone who thinks that they must live by them or else they are doomed to damnation. When someone tries to keep the commandments as a condition of being accepted by God, they are set up for constant failure and guilt and shame, which are the emotions that cause most sicknesses in the physical body. But if you will not make that mistake, then hearing the "Ten Words" will be part of your preparation to usher in the Living Word of God. So, are you ready to hear it right?

Yes, I will listen to it as if I was at camp and my loving dad sent me a list to help me stay out of danger.

As you will see it later, there is more to this. But for now this is the list that could help humanity to stay out of spiritual, mental, and physical trouble, while they are still in a state of separation, away from the presence of God, in this world. Here it is:

No other gods - No idolatry - No vain talk about God - Remember to rest regularly - Respect parents - No murdering - No adultery (breaking hearts) - No stealing - No lying (double-dealings) - No lusting (for the stuff that belongs to others).

That's it? You were right; it is short and to the point. A list like this from a loving dad would be much appreciated. I would definitely try to follow these important words. I don't see anything wrong with the Ten Commandments in this context.

The Word of God is always for our good. However when it is presented in the context of the "good-evil" misunderstanding, it changes into a "good-evil" message of impossible demands and horrid fears of messing up. To stay with the analogy of the note from the loving dad, if, instead of reading your father's words yourself, you would let an angry chaperon read it to you, who added his own interpretation of doom and gloom to the list, to make sure you are put into your place of submission to his authority, you could be mislead by this man's fear-tactics, and wonder what got into your dad, and consequently have an awful time at camp.

Yeah, I can see that. Like a good advice that is garnished with so much negative nonsense added to it, that one forgets what the point of it was in the first place. But let me ask you this, would we be all right if we could keep those commandments?

Yes, we would, but we never could. It is impossible to keep the Ten Commandments no matter how hard one may try. The only way one can live by those words is if one has spiritual and mental powers that overcome the gravity of the "good-evil" mindset. From this alone, you can see that the Ten Commandments were never given to be kept as a condition to earn good favors from God.

Well, then what were they given for?

For one, the Ten Commandments would teach cause and effect, give guidelines for social co-operation, etc. but most importantly the effect of God's written word would remind mankind of a better possibility for life. The result of such a constant reminder would keep a hope alive for the restoration of something that they lost. This longing is the preparation of mankind to desire to be restored to their original character and purpose. That longing for a Savior, who would one day appear and restore the Kingdom of God on earth and lead the children back to the Father, would stir with each failure of keeping the law. Humanity knows instinctively that only something bigger than them can bring order to their chaos.

I feel like a child at camp who longs to see the one who wrote that note. Who not only wants to read the note from Dad, but longs to be home, reunited with the loving father again...or at least yearns for Dad to show up at camp, just out of nowhere.

Then you are ready to hear the following. The grand preparation for the Living Word is accomplished in you. It is said that unless you become like a child, you cannot see the Kingdom of God (John 3:3; Mark 10:15). Which is what is happening with you while you are listening to John's account about Christ. Your eyes of faith are ready to open.

I will see God?

"No one has seen God at any time. The only begotten Son, who is in the bosom of the Father, He has declared Him" (John 1:18, NKJV).

Oh, I see. So it is Christ who will tell me about the Father?

Yes. And much, much more. He will lead you into all truth; he will be with you, like a very good big brother would. And in addition to that role, he personally will be everything you need on your way toward home. All you have to do is ask. Those who seek, find (John 12:44–50; 14:10–14).

Alright, I ask to find what I am looking for. I wonder what would Christ do if I were to walk up to him now.

He would simply ask you: "What do you seek?" (John 1:38, NKJV).

I would tell him that I wanted to see where God was.

He would answer you: "Come and see" (John 1:39, NKJV) and make you realize that God is only a turn away from you. All you have to do to find God is turn. You could talk to Christ as if he was with you where you are.

Then I wonder what Jesus would tell me? I wonder if he would know me, recognize me, you know, the way I really am…"warts and all."

He would look at you and tell you who you

used to be (pause to think and remember) or who you thought you were. But he would not dwell on the "warts and all." Rather, he would give you a new name. This, you would recognize the moment your heard it, for it is the same name that has been written in your heart from eternity, before you were born into this world (pause to listen).

I would be so thrilled. Actually I am thrilled right now...as if this really just happened. I can even feel a joyousness that I have not felt since I was a kid. I used to think I knew who I was then...(reader, do you remember?) but then I forgot...I guess. I would so much like to stay in this place of happiness with this invisible yet very real person, who just reminded me of the best thoughts about my life and what I used to hope for my future. I know if I stayed in his company, I could be what I used to dream about being as a child.

The feeling you have from that dream is your hint for your original name. This seemingly new name was just restored to you by Christ, whom you can now hear better and better. God is here with you, and now you know that this is truth. This is what faith is all about.

What would Christ say if I begged him to let me always be with him?

Why don't you listen yourself, and get your answer from God?

I don't know how to "get it."

Think about what you want to know again. Got it? Now take it to God by believing that God is with you.

Do you mind if I shut my eyes? Okay, I am doing it…I am asking Christ what to do (pause).

Now, what is Christ telling you to do? (Pause.)

This is amazing! I heard the Word telling me clearly: "Follow Me." (John 1:43, NKJV).

And what is your response?

I hear you God! And I believe you…and I will follow you with all my heart, soul, mind, and strength.

So, how do you feel now? (Take a moment to get in touch with your feelings.)

I feel like I am in the presence of great joy. I am basking in the goodness of this moment. I cannot tell you how much I appreciate you helping

me to hear the Living Word of God. It is as if God came inside of my being... But is that even possible?

Well, from now on, you have to go to the source of all possibilities for your answers. Remember, the Bible is the written Word, and now that you can hear the Living Word and you chose to follow Christ, you will know how to access all the knowledge that you would ever need.(1 John 2:20; 24–27). The one who is with you knows all things. All you have to do is ask, and you will receive abundantly. As Christ leads you forward on your journey homeward, you will be in his company at all times (John 14:26).

What if I forget or get distracted?

You may, but Christ never gets distracted... God is always with you (Deuteronomy 31:6). When you get distracted, those will be the times to practice bouncing right back into God's presence. In his presence is fullness of joy (Psalm 16:11), therefore you will always know when you are straying even a little bit. A lack of joy is a warning to you that you are way off. Paying attention to the way you feel at all times is a good way to watch over your steps. One of the inspired writers recommends that we "walk in love" (Ephesians 5:2, NKJV) which is another way of saying pay attention to your intentions.

I feel a ravenous hunger to know more about God. Don't get me wrong, I do believe what you are saying, but I just want to know all these things for myself. So, tell me, how did you find out so much about God?

Here a little, there a little…many years of learning from the written Word, sometimes through circumstances, and at times from others who had a good word for me from God…I have learned to let God lead me in the discovery. I have developed a habit of taking notes of the insights that God gives me. That has been very helpful. Telling people about God is also a wonderful way to learn when there is sincere interest; like it is right now, with you. This has been a wonderful experience for me too, because I had a chance to witness the Word of God restoring your life to the fullness of joy that makes it worth living. In a way, God's "Word became flesh" as I had the privilege of witnessing divine joy manifesting in you. You look wonderful in your physical appearance. The glory of God is shining in your face. I am glad that we had this conversation.

Oh, me too! The only thing I can't understand is why have I waited so long to "get" this? Why was I or why are people so fearful of the invisible realities?

Because most of us are lacking the experience of such a realm. As long as we are trying to explain everything based on the physical realm, we have to scratch our heads to make sense of the world as we see it. Even a blade of grass is unexplainably complex, let alone our humanity. And as long as we are lacking the connection with the Spirit of God, we will always feel out of balance, therefore fearful of the unknown. When we are searching for answers in the physical realm, to remedy our misaligned condition, we are attempting to find the answers in the wrong place. The answers are emanating from the spiritual realm, and through the mental realm we get glimpses of what we need to know in order to be balanced in all of our faculties as human beings. Now you know that once you were willing and then enabled, to connect with the Spirit of God, the living Christ came to lead you into all truth. Now you are on the highway that leads to God's presence every time. As you learn to move in and out of this invisible realm, after a while you realize that potentially, you were always in the presence of God…you just did not know it before. The same is true with other people. As soon as your experience of life becomes a harmonious blending of all the realms in perfect order and unity, you will be like a lighthouse to the people around you. As you enjoy your union with Christ, others will be drawn to that joy, causing an ever expanding harmony among mankind. That is what atonement (At-One-ment) is about, here on earth. Your inspired words and deeds will accomplish much in the lives of others.

I wish to speak inspired words also that others would understand. I have heard about Christ before, and rejected his Word many times. I am so sorry about that now. What a waste that was!

Nothing is ever wasted. God's Word never comes back void. God always accomplishes the greater purpose…even if it takes a while. The seed of life came to you over and over again, and it may have landed on a hard heart…

Yeah, hard like a flint. I used to have no use for religious talk or the Bible. I am surprised by this wonderful result of our conversation and this astonishing change that just sprang to life in me.

However, now I feel bad about how I treated those who talked to me about God in the past like they were dirt.

Instead of feeling bad, allow me to offer you a little story to facilitate understanding about the past. Let us picture a high cliff that is nothing but rock and slate. A tiny seed carried by the wind, lands in a little crack. The little seed is softened by the rains, nurtured by the sun, and soon springs up into a sprout. But because there is no soil to send its root into, it dies. Then another seed lands in the same crack, and the process is repeated over and over again for a long time, seemingly wasting many seeds that never make it past the sprouting stage. However after each dead sprout, a minute amount of wasted matter is left behind. The wind never tires; there are more seeds coming and dying in a seemingly senseless cycle. But one day, a little sprout sends out its rootlets and finds the rich fertile humus to cling to, that was created by the decaying seedlings of earlier times. So it is with the words spoken to you earlier. Even though they could not take root in your heart, they left behind a substance that became the fertile soil of faith in you now. With God nothing is ever wasted.

Well, that makes me feel much better about what I think could happen to me when I tell others about my new life with God. Even if I am treated like dirt, I can see that God can use even that for the greater good. Will I become like one of those wide-eyed people with the perpetual smile, telling everybody about the "secret to happiness"... I mean, do I have to?

Don't worry about having to tell anything to anybody. Your transformed joyful life will speak to others much better than religious hype or a theological dissertation. God arranges the divine encounters. Your part is to stay in the joy of the Lord. That will strengthen you to live in an authentic way and speak only what God inspires you to say. Stay away from arguing with others about what you believe. You don't have to prove your faith to anybody.

But what about all the other issues that people used to argue about with me? Tell me, how did you find the Way? Are there really other ways to God? Tell me about your search and what you know about the many ways that claim to lead to God also.

Certainly, there are as many ways as there are individuals searching for the real meaning of life. There are countless paths and there are many lifestyles to choose from in our quest for the abundant life.

What I have observed in my life and in the lives of others is that with these endless varieties and choices, there are potential dead-end streets and disappointed hopes also. The overabundance of options is not necessarily helpful in finding our individual way, especially when the focus of our desire is to find God.

There is an avalanche of material out there and a plethora of voices that clamor for our attention on this topic. We could be kept busy for a lifetime, just by examining all the options that the many leaders of different persuasions offer, without ever entering the highway to God.

It was with great relief, after many years of uncertainty about which way to follow, when I finally gave an honest try to understand the words of Christ on this subject.

This highway was described by Jesus with a mind-boggling figure of speech, when he answered those who asked him:

"...how can we know the way?" (John 14:5 b, NKJV).

He said:

"I Am the way..." then he added the never before offered revelation to those who longed to be rescued from a doubting mindset. Christ extended the divine invitation not only to find, but to identify with the way to the heart of God. He gave further details about this eye-opener when he declared:

"I Am the way, the truth and the life. No one comes to the Father except through Me" (John 14:6, NKJV).

I can believe that is the absolute truth now. But just moments ago, with my old mindset, I had no tolerance for statements like that. Without understanding what Christ really means, His words sound bewildering. Don't you agree?

At first, this seemed way too exclusive to me, too. I used to live in a world where being right was equated with political correctness. Initially I misunderstood the statement of Christ as a limiting elitism.

I was aware of the many voices that promised success, (the millions, the health, the toys, the prominence, the relationships, the right religion, the positions of god-like authority, etc.) and I have examined many alternatives and philosophies that our wonderful smorgasbord-like world offers. From the ridiculous to the "close, but not quite," I was inundated with ideas and the urgings to join with the different divisions of the like-minded groups. Can you relate?

Oh yes, I have done my homework on the subject as well.

I was mystified as to who could be trusted in this steady stream of diverse possibilities. After years of watching the circular pattern of mental fads, I realized that there will be no end to my endless demand for answers or to the supply of half-solutions.

Do you remember the times when someone else was telling you "the answer" that you had to know or else you would miss the boat?

Do I remember? It seems like that is all you hear these days...the "secret of the ages" perpetually rediscovered by some starry-eyed seekers who assure us that we, the human race, are the creators of the universe. And if I did not crack up laughing at that—as I look into the mirror—I would be kept busy forever by this or that "new movement" while attempting to build a pedestal for myself.

And so it goes, we are elevated to dizzying heights by one belief system, just to be browbeaten by another that asserts that we are nothing more than evolved slime.

The combinations seem endless when it comes to conjuring the "one size fits all" philosophy or religion. Like waves, these suggestions come and go. They are rediscovered, repackaged and sold to the hungry masses who do not understand that these ideas have been around since the genesis of human existence, promising fulfillment yet delivering at best, only temporary relief. And when the followers of these factions find themselves lacking true fulfillment, that is when disillusionment hits; that is when followers of man find themselves in bondage rather than in the promised freedom.

So that is why you have not asked me to join a church yet?

Let me assure you: I will not try to make you believe in a system, or compel you to join anything. There was nothing that I or anyone could have done to work out the steps to achieve your genuine connection with God. In reality there are no steps to take or works to do.

Then how come every group I can think of has some special prescriptions for their followers?

The specific works prescribed by different groups, promise exclusive favors from God. But in my experience, eventually all such efforts end in frustration and exasperated or quiet rebellion against the ever changing and inconsistent rules of man.

I am not interested in convincing you to follow me or to do what I did to find God.

God is the one who initiated it all. And God is the one who restored your connection. It is not what I said that made it happen; it was what you heard and believed that was of utmost importance. Therefore, instead of telling you what to do, I simply presented to you what I have come to believe as unshakable and practical truth for me. Then it was up to you to process what you heard. What mattered most in our conversation is whether you were willing to let the truth make the journey from your mind to your heart. That is the place where the living God is revealed to each individual. Mind consent is the beginning of the road, but the abundant life flows from the heart atoned with God.

I want to tell my family and friends about this. So what is the long story in a nutshell?

You are created by God, loved by God even in the state of spiritual disconnection. You are cherished and pursued by God until you hear the call and turn toward the Lover of your soul. Atonement is inevitable as soon as you are ready. Everything is in perfect divine order from the beginning.

Yeah, but nobody would want to hear that. They would holler: "Unfair!" How could I explain what went wrong?

Nothing went wrong! The fall of man is part of the "big picture." God is not wringing his hands about our sins. Our state of lacking God's love is the very disparity that generates the desire to be restored to unity with God. The triumph of divine love is in joyful co-creative agreement. Such a connection cannot be mandated, forced, or manipulated.

Aren't we glad!

Yes! We are free to chose, we are free to love, and we are also free to choose when.

When?

Yes, the only question is timing. Because all creation will want love sooner or later…it is the very purpose of our existence.

How will humanity finally get it?

The same as you did today. Your eternal connection was rediscovered in your turning to God. That is what the word "repent" means (Acts 3:19).

You were invited to turn to God. And when you did, at that moment the stigma of your disconnection was rendered null and void and times of refreshing (simulating, revitalizing, energizing, inspiring revival) came to you from the Lord.

Do you see now why neither I nor anyone else could "make you believe" successfully? And even if somebody would try and you would settle for "make believe" religion for the moment, you would know that something was still missing.

Well, now I know that "that something" in reality is...some-one. This is a most unexpected revelation to me. Christ is not only real but I sense his presence with me...right here...in my heart. This is the most awesome powerful experience I have ever had. I love feeling like this. I want to sing and dance!

This is what the Bible refers to as the "joy of the Lord"...there is a great celebration going on in the invisible realm of God. (Luke 15:7) This feeling is the source of your strength from now on. You are connected to the unlimited supply of God's love for you. (Psalms 28:7)

That is exactly how I feel right now. I am so at peace and content suddenly. I hope this will last. Which brings me to a question about how to make sure that my relationship with God stays this wonderful?

John 15:1–17 is a good place to get the idea about how that happens. It may surprise you when you read the invitation to that endless union that assures your steady growth and fruitfulness.

Alright then, I will read everything that you have recommended so far. But let me ask you this. Will I be okay by myself or will I need somebody, some minister to help me along as I read?

I mentioned earlier a scripture in I. John, chapter two. That passage gives you a clear understanding about what the word anointing has to do with the knowledge that you need to not only understand what to do but also how to minister to others. After reading it you may even realize that you could be a candidate for such a privileged lifestyle as well.

Are you saying that any believer can minister to others?

Yes. According to what the believer knows from experience. The hear-say method is not effective when ministering to others.

According to what I know at this point there is very little I could do. What is the modus operandi of a true minister?

A true minister is a voluntarily emptied vessel, who is joyfully and expectantly committed to hunger and thirst for God alone, eagerly waiting for the Holy Spirit to fill and then overflow with divine inspiration from the super-natural realm to others. Be it holy love, wisdom, revelation, miracles, etc. these supernatural gifts are offered to whosoever is willing to internalize them. Any one of us can allow God's character and purpose to flow unhindered from the spiritual realm to the physical. The result of such collaboration with God's intent is guaranteed to bring forth a much needed service to mankind. True ministers are of great value to all, whether they are recognized or not for their role in the world.

You are one of those…right? What did it take you to become of such value?

As a speaker I have learned some unique lessons about who is who and who is doing what when it comes to ministering to others.

For years I have experienced the gratifying responses from those who attend my meetings. It used to be so thrilling to "count the heads" of those who responded favorably to my message about the abundant life. Once we counted past our first thousand "decisions" for Christ (which means in Christian jargon, that all those people claimed that they had made the connection with God), I really thought that my life was finally worth something. How marvelous that elation was! Thinking of all those changed lives, I felt that at last I was validated and on purpose. The only problem with that validation is that it is not from God.

I could have told you that. No offence, but counting heads sounds more like an ego-trip than helping others to find God.

You've got that right! Okay, so I fell for a substitute joyride into the praise of people…but I knew that something was out of order. I was learning an important lesson about how it feels to be admired for being a "godly woman." Then one day I realized that the drive of even the holiest of purposes can derail us from the way to God's heart. Before I got lost in the act, God simply called me to enter his rest and stop working so hard. I was reminded once again that it was not up to me to convict anybody of their lack of relationship with God and neither was it my job to convince others of God's reality. God can do that much better than any of us zealous ministers. Oh, how wonderful it is to be free from that drive to change other people!

Now, my number one focus is my relationship with God first and foremost. Yes, holy selfishness...the most essential attitude in being of any real service to anyone.

I appreciate your honesty.

And why do you think am I telling you about this?

To let me see that you are human?

I assumed that you knew that already. Well, the reason I am telling you this is because I want you to see that following even the most sincere leaders is a risky way to go. We can be off from time to time, as we are forever expanding our knowledge of the Most High. None of us are a good choice to be leaders of followers. That does not mean to disrespect or disvalue the work that they do. Every religious leader has an urge that can be harnessed for good by the Spirit of God. Every congregation has the potential to let God take over and accomplish what is impossible with man alone.

Are you telling me after all that there are still some good places to join with other believers?

Of course there are. And if you really want to, you will find one that is just right for you. It may be in a traditional building, it may be in a home or a tiny meeting with a handful of people.

So you do not prefer one denomination over another?

Every denomination has a valid reason to exist in that each fraction (which is what the word means) is a particle of the whole in some way. It is up to you to match your heart's desires with what each of these groups have to offer and then decide whether to join or not. As long as you remember that your allegiance is not to a denomination but to God, you will remain free to follow the leading of the Spirit.

But how can I make sure to choose the right place for me?

Ask and God will show you a place of gathering

with others, where you will sense the presence of divine love. An assembly like that will allow God to be God in your life. You will not want to miss meeting with such a group on a regular basis. It is truly beneficial to be with people who are filled with God's love. It is worth seeking and finding such a fellowship as soon as possible...but do not try to hurry it even if it takes a while. Consider it a fun adventure. Remember, you are never alone or at the mercy of others for company. God is with you at all times, so there is no hurry to join any place.

So then why even bother?

Because when you are ready, it will serve you well to be in the company of those who are traveling on the same road from glory to glory. You will also find great satisfaction in supporting others on this exciting journey toward eternity.

But how can I be of any service to anyone?

The best service any of us can offer to our fellow brothers and sisters is to point their attention in the direction of Christ, the one who can safely lead everyone through this amazing time-space experience, right into eternity with God. Another way you can be of service to others is by living your authentic life with God and when somebody asks you about the peace and joy, to tell them what is true for you. And last but certainly not least, you can support others by letting them make their choices, even if they seem different from yours, while you are upholding their triumphant image in your prayers.

I can see that clearly now…thank you for doing just that for me. I appreciate you letting me find out what the best choice is for me. I made my choice. I will follow Christ…or even better than that, I will just stay tuned into God's presence. I may even get a Bible, now that I know the Author…

That sounds like a good plan. So how do you feel now?

Wonderful!…similar to the feeling of being in love.

Then we have arrived at our destination.

This is a good place indeed.

Glory to God!

(Author's note)We have come a long way. As you, dear reader, followed along this conversation, it is my hope that you now have the Way, the Truth, and the Life as your authentic experience. Let me know if you "got it," or more accurately, if you "got God."

You may want to reread this section again, with a Bible at your side, to look up the references in the parenthesis for yourself. God may want to show you other things while you are at it.

And if you feel inspired to do so, take notes on the pages of this book. It is fine with me.

I enjoyed "sitting" under our wonderful imaginary tree with you. But if we happened to take a walk across that beautiful bridge instead, I am sure you are enjoying the new view of your future ahead with God. Either way, it was my pleasure sharing this conversation with you. I was in the best possible company while I was writing and the One with me promised to accompany every reader of this book as well. If this benefited you, share it with others, and may the blessings of God be multiplied to you.